QUIETLY CONFIDENT

How to think, feel and communicate calmly and confidently in situations that matter to you.

Terry Gillen

COPYRIGHT

WELCOME TO QUIETLY CONFIDENT

Have you ever watched a television talent show and come to the conclusion that some people have more confidence than their ability deserves? Conversely, you might know people who have far less confidence than their potential justifies. You, yourself, might find that you can be confident in some situations but not in others.

Even people whose confidence matches their ability can usefully learn more about confidence so that it can keep pace with their growing development - and, of course, the more they know about this fascinating subject, the more they can help others develop their own confidence.

Confidence *is* a fascinating subject. It pivots on what happens in your head and, when you stand back and look objectively at what happens in your 100,000,000,000 brain cells and between your 3,200,000,000 kilometres of dendrites, it is wonderful, sometimes worrying but always mind boggling.

You will find *Quietly Confident* interesting, intriguing and thought-provoking. To be valuable to you, however, it also needs to be practical.

So, as you read on, you will be able to choose from a range of tried and tested tips that will help you **think** confidently and **behave** confidently - by working on the suggestions that register with you most, you will be able to combine your thinking *and* your behaviour in a powerful way that will provide cumulative benefits – for you and those around you.

Enjoy the journey.

Terry Gillen

Terry is a sought-after consultant, trainer and author providing practical guidance on subjects that help people in both their personal and professional lives. You can find out more at www.terrygillen.net

ESSENTIAL TERMS

Even though I have written this book in laypersons' terms, a small amount of 'jargon' provides a time-saving shorthand. Here is a list of the main terms used in **Quietly Confident** so that you can see how I use them and, as you read them, begin learning about confidence. (Some explanations use terms that appear elsewhere in this section. Those words are italicised.)

Association Your brain's tendency to: a) 'filter in' similar things when receiving information and b) to recall similar memories when thinking about something. Consequently, when you feel negative, you tend to notice or think about negative things and when you feel positive, you tend to notice or think about positive things. (See *filter*.)

Behaviour How you act, speak, gesticulate, move, what you say, etc. (It does not imply judgement as in 'good behaviour' or 'bad behaviour'.)

Body language What you communicate with your facial expression, tone of voice, posture, gestures, etc.

Catch 22 situation Based on the novel by Joseph Heller, a 'Catch 22' situation is one from which you cannot escape because of contradictory rules. For example, you want to behave more confidently but believe that you can only do so when you feel confident – but you don't feel confident because you cannot behave confidently.

Challenging situation A situation or experience that takes you out of your *comfort zone*.

Comfort zone A situation or experience that, because of your familiarity with it, does not present an undue challenge. Note

- a comfort zone does not have to be pleasant, just familiar, something to which you are accustomed.

Conscious Thinking of which you are aware and, usually, can control. The human brain is normally only comfortable processing one conscious thought at a time. (See *subconscious*.)

Cumulative effect The effect of adding small, often unnoticed, quantities over a long period. (See *tipping point*.)

Dendrites Long branching structures that form part of brain *neurons*. If you stretched out all the dendrites in your brain, you would have a line 3,200,000,000 kilometres long.

Drain behaviour Behaviour that depresses the mood of other people.

Environment What is around you (the countryside, buildings, furnishings, pictures, people, conversations, television and radio programmes, movies, music, newspapers, magazines, etc) that transmits subtle messages to your subconscious.

Fight or flight response A survival mechanism programmed into the primitive part of your brain that, when it picks up the slightest hint of a possible threat, prepares your mind and body for immediate defensive behaviour (counter-attacking or defending, fighting or fleeing).

Filter A mechanism in your *subconscious* that alters incoming information from your five senses by a) deleting information about which it decides you do not need to be consciously aware, b) distorting information to make it fit your current *paradigms* and *programs* and c) generalising information so that associated *paradigms* and *programs* can be applied more widely.

Firing threshold The ease with which information is transmitted from one combination of *neurons* to another. New behaviours and new ways of thinking can be difficult because the associated neurons have a high firing threshold; habitual behaviours and habitual ways of thinking are easy because the associated neurons have a low (established) firing threshold.

Framing How you perceive a situation. Depending on your paradigms, programs and mood, you could perceive a situation as controllable, stimulating, exciting, worrying, uncontrollable or frightening. By deliberately changing how you 'frame' a situation, you can change how you perceive it and, hence, how you think and feel about it. (See *reframing*.)

Gremlin A mischievous fictional character said to cause machinery, computers, etc to malfunction. Most of us have a mental gremlin causing our brain to malfunction (eg *frame* incoming information negatively, psyche us down instead of psyche us up).

Habit A way of thinking or behaving that has been repeated so often that the associated neural network has a very low firing threshold – so low that the thoughts/behaviours can be performed subconsciously, that is, without conscious intervention. Being well within your *comfort zone*, habitual ways of thinking and behaving can be difficult to change.

Imaginary dress rehearsal The process of imagining your behaviour and feelings in a future situation.

Inner dialogue See *self-talk*.

Mentor A trusted adviser. With the right tips and understanding you can convert your mental gremlin into a mental mentor.

Modelling The process of copying the thoughts, feelings and behaviours of someone who is competent in a given situation, increasing the chances that you perform competently in that situation too.

Motivation The force, mostly within you, that causes you to do something. Motivation can be 'away from' (you are motivated to avoid something) or 'towards' (you are motivated to achieve something). This can affect confidence if you *frame* a situation negatively or *filter* in problems rather than opportunities.

Neuron A nerve cell and core component of the nervous system (mostly the brain and spinal cord). Your brain contains about 100,000,000,000 neurons that process and transmit information by electrical and chemical signalling and connect to each other (combine) via *dendrites* to form neural networks. (See *plasticity*.)

Paradigms A model of thinking; your understanding of how something is or should be. Inherited from your *environment* (especially parents and other influential people), paradigms tend to be deep within your subconscious and, consequently, can be difficult to change (paradigm paralysis) despite contradictory evidence because, like the systems programming in a computer, most of us are unaware that paradigms even exist. When they do change, however, the difference can be significant (paradigm shift).

Pay-off The emotional benefit of remaining within the *comfort zone* of your current *paradigms*, *habits*, etc.

Perception What something or a situation looks like from our viewpoint; what we think of as reality after incoming information has been *filtered*.

Perceptual position How people perceive a situation from their viewpoint. In a conversation between you and another person, for example, there are three perceptual positions: 1 yours, 2 the other person's and 3 that of an independent observer (imaginary or real). We have the ability to switch perceptual positions. When you do so deliberately, it is easier to understand other people and to *reframe* and *model*.

Plasticity The ability of brain neurons to form new neural networks (combinations). This is very useful when shifting *paradigms* and developing new *habits*.

Program Similar to a paradigm but more about you as a person. Conceptually, they can be easier to change because, as with our computer's programs, we are accustomed to installing updates, applying 'fixes', doing virus checks, etc.

Radiator behaviour Behaviour that lifts and lightens the mood of other people.

Received meaning The interpretation of our communication by the person receiving it. Contamination from our body language (tone of voice, for example) or their framing or filter could result in them 'receiving' communication different from what we thought we 'transmitted'.

Reference group A group of people to whom you compare yourself. Your choice of reference groups is usually subconscious and is made to confirm existing *paradigms* and *programs*. Depending on the group, the comparison can make you feel positive or negative about yourself.

Reframing Deliberately changing how you perceive a situation so that your thoughts, feelings and behaviour can be more effective. (See *framing* and *perceptual position*.)

Resources The abilities, skills, competencies and *states* that help you achieve something. When you are aware of your many resources, it is easier for you to access them when you need them.

Rights and responsibilities A 'right' is something to which you feel you are entitled, such as *to be listened to* or *to be treated with respect*. Every right carries a corresponding responsibility, such as *to listen to others* or to *treat others with respect*. As rights and responsibilities affect both our feelings and our behaviour, acknowledging them makes confident thinking and confident behaviour easier.

Risk The possibility of being harmed or suffering loss. Risk is a combination of the *likelihood* of something happening and the *consequences* if it does happen. People who lack confidence typically allow their imaginations to overestimate risk by focussing on (and often exaggerating) the *consequences* and ignoring the *likelihood*. Assessing risk objectively is empowering as well as safe.

Sat-nav A device, often found in cars that, by using global positioning satellite technology, directs you to a destination you have programmed into it. We all have the equivalent of a mental sat-nav that directs our behaviour according to the *programs* and *paradigms* programmed into us. Unlike a real sat-nav, however, your mental sat-nav operates subconsciously, directing your thoughts and behaviour silently and subtly.

Self-talk The conversations and chatter in your subconscious. When controlled by your mental gremlin, self-talk is counter-productive. When you become consciously aware of it, you can intervene and make your self-talk positive.

State Your mood; how you feel. You can use *reframing, perceptual positions, modelling* and positive *self-talk* to change your 'state' and thereby think and behave more effectively. Even your posture and breathing can affect your state.

Subconscious Thinking of which you are not consciously aware. The vast majority of your thoughts, *paradigms, programs, habits,* etc (especially those controlling your day-to-day behaviour) are subconscious.

Thermostat A device that regulates room temperature by monitoring it and automatically turning on, or turning off, heating/ air conditioning so that room temperature stays within a few degrees of the programmed (comfortable) level. Some people have a subconscious 'mood thermostat' that works in conjunction with their *filter, self-talk* and choice of *reference groups* to maintain their programmed mood.

Tipping point The moment when small, cumulative additions produce a big change. For example, the moment, when adding small quantities of cooking ingredients to kitchen scales, the cumulative weight of the ingredients suddenly makes the scales tip. Cumulative learning and the persistent application of new behaviours have a similar effect on our confidence and the quality of our lives.

Chapter 1

Something worth thinking about

DESCARTES UPDATED

In 1644, the French philosopher and mathematician, Rene Descartes, came up with the immortal words, *'I think, therefore I am'* - sometimes written, *'I think, therefore I exist'*. He rationalised that being consciously aware of the fact that he was thinking was proof that he existed.

Thinking might prove you exist but don't you want to do more than exist? Don't you want, and have a right to, a fulfilling life? To do that, you need to take Descartes' statement a step further and be more aware of *what* you think about and *how* you think about it because, as you will discover in this book, the *what* and the *how* of your thinking affect the kind of existence you have.

What you think about and how you think about it determine the way you experience life and, consequently, they affect the quality of your life.

THE QUALITY OF YOUR LIFE

Consider just a few of the things that add 'quality' to life and make it more fulfilling - satisfying relationships, a generally positive outlook, a positive response to the inevitable problems you encounter, hobbies you make time for, work that adds to your sense of worth, a worthwhile pursuit you invest time in, a willingness to help others and contributing to society, etc.

The quality of your life depends on what you do - your behaviour. Behaviour (other than automatic responses such as pulling your hand away from something hot) is, to one extent or another, preceded by thought. Deciding what to have for breakfast, juggling priorities so that you can watch that important television programme or planning how to broach a tricky topic with a work colleague are behaviours that involve thinking.

How you *think* determines how you *behave* and, as you will see shortly, the quality of your thinking affects much more than your breakfast, television viewing or whose turn it is to make the coffee.

The quality of your thinking affects a lot!

It affects the kind of person you are, your perception, your attitudes, values and beliefs, the subjective world you inhabit, your relationships to things and to people; your experiences; whether you are sad, pessimistic, frustrated, anxious, restless, pitied and avoided as bad company or whether you are happy, optimistic, fulfilled, relaxed, peaceful, admired and sought after as good company.

It also affects your perception of yourself, your outlook and your relative level of confidence.

All this is a consequence of what you think about and how you think about it.

So when was the last time you thought about your thinking? This is more than just becoming consciously aware that you are thinking about something; it means considering your thoughts, cleaning them up, dumping those old habitual thoughts that are past their 'use by date', identifying the ones with negative knock-on effects, consciously changing them and deliberately rehearsing and practising those that prove productive

POWERFUL POSSIBILITIES

Understanding what you think about and how you think about it are vital steps in the direction you take in the journey of life. On one hand, you avoid serious problems.

Lack of confidence goes hand in hand with a tendency towards low self esteem, stress, procrastination and pessimism.

This combination, according to research, results in more visits to the doctor, a weaker immune system, lower survival rates from serious illness and earlier mortality than the statistics would suggest.

On the other hand, you can be happier, more sociable, have more friends, achieve more, relax more, be more respected and feel better about yourself.

These are powerful possibilities.

WHAT THIS MEANS TO YOU

What those possibilities might mean to you depends on your starting point.

- Your 'default setting' might be pessimistic or melancholy and you want to feel happier.

- You know you have the potential to achieve more but 'something inside you' seems to be holding you back.

- You might have sufficient confidence to handle many situations, especially those with which you are already familiar, but you want to reach out and apply the same level of confidence to more challenging situations.

- You might feel that your level of confidence is displayed in a way that makes some people feel uncomfortable and, consequently, you want to achieve a better balance.

- You might just want to understand the subject better so that you can help a friend or loved one whose confidence needs strengthening.

Whatever *Quietly Confident* means to you, the results can range from helpful and self-affirming to fundamental and life-changing.

HOW CONFIDENT ARE YOU?

One of the problems with low confidence is that it can feel normal.

Have you ever assessed your own level of confidence? Checking it can confirm whether your level of confidence is ok or whether it needs to be dusted off, cleaned up and revitalised.

The following questionnaire will not tell you if you are confident or not (that has to be your decision); neither will it give you a score quantifying your level of confidence (that is too open to misinterpretation).

You will know, as you answer these questions and reflect on your answers, if your confidence is at the general level you want.

1. How frequently do you dwell on, and get upset by, negative stories or the news?

2. How frequently do you do what you feel 'compelled' to do, or what you 'must' do or 'should' do rather than what you really want to do?

3. To what extent are you concerned about what people might think about you?

4. How easily are you persuaded to do what you would prefer not to do? How susceptible are you to peer pressure?

5. To what extent do you consistently put the needs of others before your own needs?

6. How often does anxiety affect your decisions, choices and actions?

7. To what extent do you give up easily? How easily discouraged are you?

8. To what extent do you avoid, or feel uncomfortable about, social events where you won't know many people?

9. To what extent do you feel self-conscious or disagree when people praise you?

10. To what extent does criticism make you feel bad?

11. Compared to other people, how sensitive are you?

12. To what extent do you avoid difficult conversations with people?

13. How often do you doubt your ability or believe it is less than that of other people?

14. To what extent do you consistently blame yourself when things go wrong?

15. To what extent do you gravitate towards negative thinking rather than positive thinking?

16. How often do you become aware that you are thinking negatively or replaying something negative in your imagination?

17. Do you have an inner voice? To what extent is it positive and empowering or negative and controlling? Do you ever wish you could shut it up?

18. To what extent do you feel that negative 'programs' are running in your brain?

19. In one sentence, how would other people describe you to a third party? How do you feel about that description?

20. To what extent do you feel you lack confidence?

21. How many times, in response to these questions, did your brain respond with a qualifying *'Yes, but...'* instead of a straight answer?

I suggest you let your answers sink in for a while. Reflect on which questions registered with you most, which answers you found most uncomfortable and which you would most like to change. That reflection will help you benefit more from the valuable ideas in this book.

QUICK START GUIDE

Keen to get started? If you want to, you can begin straight away with any of these seven suggestions:

1 **Walk, speak and generally do things with a little more pace and purpose.** Behave *as if* you were (even more) confident, positive and optimistic. Breathe a bit more slowly and deeply with more emphasis on the inhale than the exhale. In the same way that an object cannot be in two places at the same time, you cannot be 'not confident' and 'confident' at the same time. When you walk, move and breathe confidently, you affect how you feel *and* how other people feel about you.

2 **Think of a situation in which your confidence feels low and see in how many ways you can reframe it.** Reframe the situation from at least three different perspectives. Ask yourself which reframe is most conducive to feeling confident and behaving confidently. Aim to do this at least twice a day.

3 Focus on at least one easy situation an hour in which you will think and/or behave confidently. Consciously thinking confident thoughts and behaving confidently continuously throughout your waking hours won't work because your conscious brain only has space for one thought at a time – and you'll probably need that space to get some work done or cross the road safely. So practise feeling and behaving confidently in brief, specific situations. This might mean making eye contact and smiling at someone as you hold a door open for them or as someone serves you in a shop. If that is already very easy for you, try accepting a compliment by saying *'Thank you'* instead of belittling yourself and/or the compliment. If that is already very easy, try something more challenging such as returning a faulty product to a shop. When you start with easy situations, you get the hang of it quickly and feel more inclined to repeat the process by behaving confidently in situations containing slightly more challenge. This frequent application, gradually 'stretching' your confident thinking and behaviour, is easier and more learning-efficient than infrequent application to very big challenges. The cumulative effect builds up surprisingly quickly.

4 Intercept negative self-talk and replace it with positive self-talk – even if you have to *pretend* you're confident. Just like everyone else, you have a voice in your subconscious that talks to you and, every now and then, you become consciously aware of it. When the voice is critical or negative, it depresses your mood, making confident behaviour more difficult. So, as soon as you become consciously aware of negative self-talk, intervene and make two changes. First, change the tone. Make it a friendlier, kinder and more positive voice. Second, make what it says more constructive, forward-looking and empowering. When you change its tone and content, you lift your mood and confident behaviour follows more naturally.

5 Allow small frustrating problems to bypass you. It's easy to get into a habit of noticing and reacting to small problems. As this habit develops, the firing threshold of the associated brain neurons lowers. You then begin *over-reacting,* even to small problems, your mood thermostat resets at a lower level and confidence becomes more elusive. Instead, stay calm. When, for example, a road hog comes out in front of you, your train is late or the computer takes a long time to boot up, just *let it go.* Please note that this is not the same as gritting your teeth and suppressing your emotions. You simply allow the problem to bypass you; *there is no emotion.* By allowing the problems to bypass your emotions, you effectively train yourself to stay calm in more challenging situations. When you are calm, it is easier to maintain control of your thoughts and behaviours. Confidence is easier.

6 Get some 'confidence coaches'. Tell some friends or colleagues what you are doing and ask them to describe what they notice about you, how you come across and what effect your behaviour has on other people in specific situations. This has several benefits: learning is more motivational when the process is shared; your 'coaches' will notice things that you don't; different 'coaches' will notice different things in different situations, providing overall comprehensive feedback; by choosing specific situations, the feedback will be specific, which is much more useful than generalised feedback.

7 Aim to make at least one person a day feel good for having come into contact with you. That contact could be a friendly 'Good morning' as you pass them in a corridor, smiling as you hold open a door for them, a genuine 'Thank you' to a shop assistant, listening unconditionally to a friend, giving a colleague specific praise and so on. This shifts the focus of your thoughts and behaviours from yourself to other people, which provides two major benefits: first, it makes it easier for you to 'get on' with feeling confident and behaving confidently (it's amazing what we can do when we stop thinking about it and just do it); second, seeing how good you make people feel makes you feel good too.

Chapter 2

Confidence, reality, chickens and spirals

IS THIS YOU?

Have you ever wondered exactly what confidence is? Do you know the traits that indicate confidence? Have you ever wondered why you can feel confident in some situations but not others? How often do you talk yourself out of feeling confident? How often do you feel anxious about what 'might' happen? Would you like to feel calm, capable and generally 'ok' most of the time? Would you like your 'default setting' to be optimistic and positive?

IN THIS CHAPTER

This chapter will help you understand important points about confidence; understanding them will help you personalise following chapters much more easily.

WHAT IS CONFIDENCE?

As confidence has many elements, it is easier to describe than define. So here is a list of the traits that indicate confidence. As you read them, you can highlight the ones that 'register' with you most.

Characteristics of Confidence

✓ Feelings of certainty, of self-reliance.

✓ A positive outlook; the positive expectation that you can do something or can learn how to do it; a feeling that things will work out ok, that you can cope with life's challenges.

✓ A rational perspective and realistic interpretation of events.

✓ An inclination to take responsibility for yourself, to ask for what you feel is reasonable, to seek help and cooperation when necessary and to be active rather than passive.

✓ A sense of self-worth; a natural entitlement to normal human rights.

✓ A feeling of being 'ok' and generally feeling content with who you are. Confidence, therefore, also links to feelings of happiness and general well-being.

These characteristics affect relationships with family, friends, neighbours and work colleagues. They also affect ambitions, dreams and destinies.

TOO MUCH CONFIDENCE

Before we go any further, we should address where confidence ends and stupidity begins. Leaping off an incredibly tall building unaided (self-reliant) believing that everything will work out well (positive outlook) might be confident but it's also stupid. A more modest example might be the many television talent shows in which some contestants seem to have a level of confidence that far exceeds their ability to entertain.

Confidence works best when it is rooted in reality – but 'reality' is not what it seems.

CONFIDENCE AND REALITY

Confidence needs to be rooted in reality - but whose reality?

How many talented singers don't enter a talent contest because their 'reality' vastly underestimates their talent, compares it to world famous entertainers or exaggerates, in their imagination, the risk of looking foolish?

Conversely, how many people do actually relish the experience of leaping off incredibly tall buildings? (They are called 'base jumpers'.) Their reality takes into account wind speed and direction, temperature, visibility, landing area, canopy dynamics, their sky-diving skills and the interpretation of fear and danger as exhilarating and life affirming.

'Whose reality?' is so central to confidence that we will explore it in more detail when we look at *Paradigms and Programming*. As we will also explore later, our individual reality is only our *perception* - and our perception is influenced by many factors such as childhood experiences, interpretation of success or failure, and the people with whom we spend time. Even the magazines we read, television programmes we watch or computer games we play affect our perception.

Our perception is our individual, subjective reality.

Objective reality, on the other hand, makes it so much easier to handle life's ups and downs.

SNAKES AND LADDERS

Like the game of *snakes & ladders*, life has ups and downs, obstacles and opportunities. This is normal. Whether someone finds life fulfilling or a burden rarely depends on their good fortune – it depends on the action they take in response to obstacles and whether they grasp, or even notice, opportunities. This requires action.

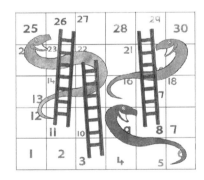

Undue pessimism and unwarranted anxiety stifle positive action. Success, however you choose to define it, requires action and action is easier when it is underpinned by confident thinking rooted in objective reality.

Confidence is a combination of thinking and behaving.

CHICKEN AND EGG

Can you behave confidently before you feel confident or will feeling confident come more easily when you behave confidently? Must one come first?

This is like asking whether it is the chicken or the egg that comes first. Confident thinking leads to confident behaviour. Confident behaviour produces better outcomes. Better outcomes alter our perception (our individual reality) making confident thinking easier and so the cycle continues.

CYCLES, SPIRALS AND POLARITY

The interplay between your thinking and your behaviour is like a spiral – one that determines whether you progress *towards* your goals,

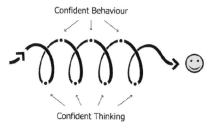

Confident Behaviour

Confident Thinking

or move *farther away* from them.

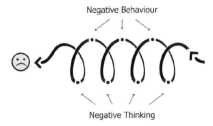

When you move towards your goals, you not only tend to behave more confidently, you think more confidently which, in turn, increases the likelihood of more confident behaviour.

When, on the other hand, you move away from your goals, your behaviour tends to be more negative and you begin thinking more negatively, increasing the likelihood of more negative behaviour.

It is as if the <u>polarity</u> of your spiral changes.

LIFE'S SPIRAL AND THE IMPORTANCE OF 'POLARITY'

This concept applies to the quality of your life.

As you progress through life, you have numerous 'everyday experiences'.

The quality of your life depends less on what happens to you and more on how you choose to interpret and respond to what happens to you.

It is your *interpretation* that determines the 'polarity' of the experience. This is especially important with 'everyday' experiences because:

- they are frequent,

- they are small enough to go unnoticed consciously but are absorbed by your subconscious,

- their effect is *cumulative*.

Changes due to numerous, small, subconscious choices creep up on us so slowly that we hardly notice their cumulative effect.

THE CUMULATIVE EFFECT AND YOUR SAT-NAV SETTING

In the same way that an aircraft a tiny two degrees off course as it flies between London and New York will end up 120 miles away from its intended destination, our everyday actions can lead to a life miles away from our intended, or desirable, 'destination'.

When we don't think about the way we think, our numerous daily 'thinking choices' can too easily lead to behaviours that have a negative cumulative effect.

On the other hand, when we intervene in our thoughts and make them work for us, our behaviours are much more likely to produce a positive, cumulative effect. This process is easier and more consistent when it is underpinned by a positive 'sat-nav setting' – one based on confident thinking.

How can you make the cumulative effect work for you? Let's put confidence under the microscope.

CONFIDENCE UNDER THE MICROSCOPE

It is worth thinking about the situations in which you want to be more confident and how much confidence you want in them. This will help you personalise the information in this book.

How much confidence do you want and in what situations do you want it?

If you are lazing on a beach trying to get a tan, you might want a temperature of x degrees. If you are a guest at a wedding, wearing formal clothes, you might prefer a cooler temperature of x minus 10 degrees. You can think of confidence in a similar, situation-specific way.

Look at these example situations and ask yourself if any of them apply to you and, if they do, how much more confidence you want in them:

- Agreeing a more equitable division of tasks at home.

- Telling a loved one how you really feel.

- Asking a neighbour to be more cooperative.

- Asserting your rights in a shop.

- Standing up for yourself at work.

- Getting the recognition and appreciation you deserve.

- Finding more 'me time'.

- Doing something you really want to do but keep putting off.

- Making a bigger contribution to society.

- 'Stretching out' and doing something more fulfilling with your life.

You probably find that, in some situations, you already have enough confidence, in some you want only a bit more and, in others, you want a lot more.

When you think of confidence in a situation-specific way, you'll notice that you can assess 'risk' much more objectively.

Risk and objective reality

When your perceived risk is too great for your level of situation-specific confidence, you become too passive. Notice the word 'perceived'; *perceived* risk and *actual* risk can be very different.

A simple and effective confidence-building step is to align perceived risk and actual risk more closely.

That is easier when you understand risk. A useful way of thinking of risk is as a combination of:

* the *consequences* of something going wrong,

* the *likelihood* of it going wrong.

Example 1

Skydiving with no training or supervision has high risk because the *consequences* of something going wrong and the *likelihood* of it going wrong are both extremely high. Skydiving strapped to a qualified instructor has much lower risk; the *consequences* of something going wrong are the same but the *likelihood* of anything going wrong is much lower. Some people who would love to try a tandem skydive won't do so because they only perceive the consequences, causing them to exaggerate the risk.

Example 2

Introducing yourself to a pleasant-looking stranger at a social gathering has virtually no risk (the likelihood of something going wrong is about average and the consequences of something going wrong are tiny) yet some people would remain passively standing on their own. They don't understand 'risk' and so exaggerate it.

SUMMARY

You will benefit if you avoid thinking of confidence as something you have or do not have. It doesn't have an 'on' or 'off' like a light switch. Think of it as situation-specific – in some situations you might need a lot of confidence while in other situations you might only need a bit. You can choose how much more you want in relation to a specific situation. That way, you will always be close enough to the security of your comfort zone to feel ok about developing your confidence.

You can:

- Think of confidence as situation-specific.

- Assess the risk in a situation objectively.

- Ask yourself, now that you have assessed the risk accurately, how much more confidence you need in that situation – or do you already have enough?

When you start thinking this way, you get more and more ideas.

Chapter 3

What's stopping you?

IS THIS YOU?

Do you ever find that certain situations make you feel unhelpfully anxious or angry? Do you ever feel anxious or angry when you reflect on a conversation you've had with someone? How frequently do you think about how you responded in a situation and feel it is similar to the way you would have responded as a child or the way one of your parents might have responded? Do you ever discover that the way you see a situation is very different from the way others see it? How often do your own thoughts sabotage your confidence? Would you like to control the confidence-sapping 'chatter' in your own brain?

IN THIS CHAPTER

Confidence is not something you have, like a possession or a muscle – it is something you feel.

Whether or not you feel confident is a function of how you think.

So, in the same way that we can often operate a machine better when we understand a little of how it works, you will be able to think more confidently when you understand some of the 'mechanics' of how your brain works.

Here is information describing **five features** of brain processing that affect your confidence.

FEATURE 1 - THE EFFECT OF EVOLUTION

For millions of years humans lived in extended family units or small tribes, hunting and gathering food to survive. The world was a risky place. There were lots of predators who regarded us as lunch and a variety of snakes, spiders and even small animals that, if we inadvertently disturbed them, could kill us. In response to these numerous threats, we evolved two survival mechanisms - *the fight or flight response* and *acceptance/reciprocity.*

Fight or flight

This response gives us an almost instant ability to respond physically (to fight or to flee) whenever we see even a small sign of a potential threat. There are four points about the fight or flight response relevant to confidence:

- It happens in the part of the brain that works incredibly quickly. It takes milliseconds for the fight or flight response to kick in.

- It happens subconsciously; conscious thinking would take far too long for us to respond rapidly enough to survive.

- It perceives something as safe *or* as a threat; there is no 'maybe' or 'benefit of the doubt'. When our subconscious perceives even the *tiniest hint* of a *potential threat*, we respond first and think later.

- It does not distinguish between a *physical threat* and an *emotional threat* or between a *real threat* and an *imagined threat*; it just responds.

Examples

Have you had any of the following experiences?

A real physical threat. You are driving along the road when another vehicle suddenly pulls out in front of you. Your foot hits the brake 'before you know it'. This is what happened. Your eyes picked up the other vehicle and sent the information to the primitive part of your brain. Your subconscious received the visual information, assessed it as a potential threat and instructed your foot to transfer from accelerator to brake. Literally half a second later you became consciously aware of the threat but, by then, your foot was already on the brake. This is rapid, intricate and marvellous cooperation between your subconscious and body without any conscious intervention. After this incident, was your heart beating quickly, were you breathing rapidly and were the palms of your hands sweating? That is the physical part of the fight or flight response.

A 'false alarm' physical threat. Have you ever been suddenly and unexpectedly startled by something like a snake, spider or scary face only to discover, a split second later, that it was actually something completely harmless – but your heart was still beating quickly, you were still breathing heavily and the palms of your hands were sweating? You had just experienced the 'respond first, think later' feature of the fight or flight response.

A real emotional threat. Have you ever been criticised by someone (say, someone in a position of authority) who emphasises their words by speaking loudly with an angry or condescending tone of voice, pointing or wagging their index finger at you? As they did so, did you feel your heart rate increasing, your palms sweating, etc? While, consciously, you knew that you were not in physical danger, your subconscious responded *as if you might be* and prepared you to fight or flee.

An imagined emotional threat. Have you ever been thinking about a future event (say, a challenging conversation) and found your heart rate increasing, palms sweating, etc? You are in no physical danger. In fact, at this stage, the conversation is only happening in your imagination. Yet your brain has triggered your fight or flight response <u>as if you were actually facing a physical threat right now</u>.

These examples cover a wide range of situations, yet to each of these situations your subconscious responded exactly the same way - preparing your brain and body to fight or flee.

Overall, we have inherited the genes of those of our ancestors who, when faced with a genuine threat, a 'false alarm' or even just an emotional 'threat', responded instantly with a big rush of adrenalin to facilitate fighting or fleeing.

It can actually be reassuring to realise that a lot of your responses in confidence-challenging situations are the result of evolution and are not proof of any inadequacy on your part.

Acceptance/reciprocity

Evolution has taught us that we are safer when we are part of a social group. After all, stragglers and loners are easier prey for predators - and those who are ostracized by the tribe quickly become stragglers and loners. Consequently, our need to be accepted is very strong.

As an accepted member of the tribe, others will share their food with you when you return empty handed as you will share your food when they return empty handed. This 'law of reciprocity' means others will look out for you and your family as you will look out for them.

It can be difficult to turn off this survival instinct even when it is no longer relevant and, if your confidence is low, you never get to watch what you want to watch on television, you let others interrupt you, take you for granted and take credit for your work. You always agree to requests for help, no matter how unreasonable, yet you feel uncomfortable asking for help yourself, no matter how reasonable.

When the 'acceptance' instinct combines with low confidence, it is easy to gravitate towards consistently putting yourself last.

Summary

The primitive part of your brain evolved to ensure survival in a primitive world. Many of its important functions are still relevant. They will keep you safe on the roads, help you foresee problems and make you a good neighbour and work colleague. They will, however, combine with your perception to affect your thinking and behaviour in situations for which they were never intended.

As survival mechanisms operate subconsciously, you will not even know it is happening; you assume the problem is you, rather than a side effect of evolution, and you slip backwards along the spiral.

All this is programmed into us before we are born. After we are born a lot of other programming gets into our brains. This is where *rule-making giants* come onto the scene.

FEATURE 2 - GIANTS AND RULES

We have mobile telephones, emails, chat rooms and social networking yet many of us still experience communication problems. How often are we more upset by *how* someone communicated rather than by *what* they communicated? How often do we know what we want to say to someone but don't know how to say it effectively?

We have been communicating since we were born yet too many of us still can't get it right in situations that matter to us.

In a way, that is the problem – we have been communicating since childhood and issues affecting confidence start early. As you developed a vocabulary, mobility and a tendency to test boundaries, you did so in a world dominated by *giants* and *rules*.

Giants

Can you remember what it was like to be a small child? Parents, aunts, uncles and school teachers were two or three times your height. They were also extremely powerful. They dispensed rewards and punishments, particularly the subtle ones like a smile, a shout, attention or temporary  ostracism. These giants occupy a hugely responsible role – often with no training in how to communicate with children. They also make and police the rules.

Rules

As adults, most of us have forgotten the vast quantity of rules around which children have to navigate.

- Many of the rules are sensible - stopping at the curb rather than running into the road is a good example.

- Many of the rules will help children comply with the norms of society - not taking other people's property without their prior permission is a good example.

- Some of the rules are a matter of parental preference, such as not putting one's elbows on the table during meals or not interrupting while an adult is talking.

- Some rules (and this causes confusion as we grow) appear only occasionally depending on what kind of day the parent has had. Behaviour from the child that was ok yesterday has suddenly transgressed a rule that has appeared out of nowhere, perhaps because the parent had a stressful day at work, and the child gets the punishment. That punishment might only be a scowl or a cross word and the parent has forgotten about it two minutes later but in a child's world, and coming from an omnipotent giant, it's a big deal – big enough to trigger the child's fight or flight response.

It has been estimated that children experience a negative to positive ratio of 30 to 1. The result is that even the children of kind, loving parents get a lot of fight or flight experiences and negative emotions during their formative years.

It gets worse!

Some parents also have rules they inherited from their parents which they pass on unquestioningly to their children.

Examples would include rules relating to religion, politics, gender roles, self discipline, ambition, social mobility, respect for self and others, attitude towards the law, self-sufficiency, socially acceptable behaviour and the rights of certain family members.

These rules are so strong and subtle they are called *paradigms* and *programs*.

FEATURE 3 - PARADIGMS AND PROGRAMS

A paradigm is *a belief, deeply embedded in your subconscious, of how things are meant to be*. Paradigms are a bit like a computer's operating system or systems programming – the software deep inside that specifies the rules to which the computer adheres.

Paradigms have a central role in every society. When an understanding of how things are meant to be is shared by most people, we feel comfortable with them because their interpretation of events is similar to ours and their behaviour is predictable. As a result, society functions better.

A program is a belief, not quite so deep in the subconscious, about yourself. A program is a bit more like the computer's software of which we are more aware and are more accustomed to updating. Paradigms and programs are, however, both 'software' affecting your behaviour.

Paradigms, programs and behaviour

Unfamiliar, outdated or misplaced paradigms do not just cause confusion, they affect behaviour.

Part of the role of parents is to pass on paradigms to their children. The parents may have never heard the word 'paradigm' but they do *know how things are meant to be.*

Example

I once suggested to some course participants that they would find their course notes more useful if they annotated them. One course participant looked shocked and said, *'You're not supposed to write in books; it's wrong'.* Further enquiry revealed that this 'rule' came from her parents' instruction not to write in school textbooks. The fact that there was a huge difference between textbooks belonging to a school that would be used by other pupils and personal course notes that belonged to the participant and would only ever be used by herself, could not penetrate the generalised and outdated paradigm.

Some paradigms are so out of date or situation-specific that they become seriously restrictive.

They are also passed on unquestioningly from 'giants' to children. I guess we shouldn't be too hard on parents. After all, they learned all that stuff from their parents, who learned it from their parents and so on – a process that has served primitive hunter-gatherers well for thousands of generations. In societies that hardly ever change, it is a very efficient mechanism. In societies that do change, however, it causes problems for individuals who want to change – even a change as personal as developing more confidence. Which raises an interesting question -

How many of us have paradigms tucked away in our subconscious that are no longer relevant?

For example, rules about gender responsibilities, career choices or kowtowing to one's workplace manager which were applicable to our parents may be well out of date or even highly restrictive when applied to a subsequent generation.

If those paradigms are programmed into us they affect our behaviour subconsciously.

And what if you also pick up paradigms from sources such as friends, music, magazines, computer games, the internet, celebrities and other 'icons', sport, jobs, etc? These aspects of your 'environment' all transmit information about how things are 'meant to be'.

We all have paradigms programmed into our subconscious. Some will stand us in good stead for the whole of our lives. Others, however, might have been relevant to us when we were children or relevant to our parents but they are now so well past their 'use by' date they are a handicap to our progress and affect our confidence.

Example

Imagine a child with older brothers and sisters. The child wants to do what its older siblings do but is told by its over-protective parents, *'You're too little. You've got to wait until you're bigger'* or *'You're too young. You must wait until you're older'*. How often does this mantra need to be repeated before it programmes the young brain? How old will the child be before she realises that she *is* big enough or old enough?

Twenty? Thirty? Never? How many opportunities will the young adult miss while waiting to be 'bigger' or 'old enough' with the inevitable erosion of confidence?

Paradigms, programs and internal tension

Paradigms and programs can cause tension. Sometimes that tension is between people and sometimes it is *within us* as individuals.

When, for example, your career paradigm is telling you to apply for promotion and your self-image program is telling you that you are not good enough to get that kind of job, it creates internal tension. It's like putting your foot on the accelerator while firmly holding on the parking brake.

Some brain software is not just about how our culture is meant to be, it is about how you are meant to be.

The effect of paradigms and programs in a single situation might not be noticeable but the **cumulative effect** of numerous, everyday situations adds up with the inevitable effect on confidence.

Deep subconscious programs beat rational conscious thoughts every time.

Paradigms and programs deep in the freezer

Have you ever checked the back of your freezer and found a packet of food long past its 'use-by' date? Do you have any qualms about throwing it out? Similarly, outdated and long-forgotten paradigms and programs can hide in the recesses of your subconscious.

It is sensible to check what out-dated paradigms and programs are hidden deep in your subconscious.

Being a human being is tricky stuff for confidence. Especially as the rules, paradigms and programs affect the way your *filter* 'fiddles' with incoming information.

FEATURE 4 - YOUR FIDDLING FILTER

Subconscious and conscious

Your subconscious is really impressive. It never sleeps, is not distracted and can multi-task like you wouldn't believe.

Examples

You might have had the common experience of becoming absorbed in a thought while driving. After several miles, you become consciously aware of your surroundings and ask yourself, *'How did I get here?'* For the last few miles, while your conscious brain was absorbed in <u>one thought</u>, your subconscious has been driving the car, listening to the engine note and changing gear, deciding how much pressure to place on the accelerator and brake pedals, operating indicators, navigating the route, obeying road signs, stopping at junctions, executing complex speed and trajectory calculations, giving that cyclist extra room because they're a bit wobbly, etc, etc. The subconscious brain's ability to process multiple strands of information is incredible - seriously incredible.

Now consider the conscious part of your brain. Have you ever been at home and gone into another room to get something, got there and forgotten what it was you went in there for? One simple thought and your conscious brain has difficulty holding onto it for a few seconds! Surprisingly, the conscious part of your brain is very limited. It only works when you are awake, is only comfortable with one thought at a time and is easily distracted. Compared to the subconscious, it can be pretty puny.

We are so aware of our conscious thoughts, we easily believe that the conscious is more powerful than the subconscious. No, it is the other way round.

The subconscious is the biggy. Even megabrains like Einstein readily admit that it is the subconscious that comes up with the real breakthroughs.

Incoming information and brain trickery

Your brain is constantly receiving information from the outside world and it can come as quite a shock to find out what tricks your subconscious can play with it.

Incoming information is picked up by one or more of your five senses - sight, sound, taste, touch and smell. Your brain monitors and processes this incoming information. The volume of incoming information is so great, however, that most of that work is done by your subconscious; if too much information reached your conscious brain, it would 'crash' like an overloaded computer.

Your subconscious brain decides <u>what</u> gets through to your conscious brain and <u>how</u> it gets through.
This process is called 'filtering'.

Filtering works like this - incoming information is picked up by your senses and transmitted to the subconscious part of your brain. The subconscious then filters the information, deciding *what* it will allow through to the conscious brain and *how* it will allow it through.

Example

Imagine you are at a party or other social gathering. People are talking in small groups. Someone in your group whispers, *'Hey, what are they talking about in the group behind you?'* You reply, *'I don't know. I can't hear what they're saying.'* (After all, there is probably a lot of noise going on.) Then someone in the group behind mentions your name as part of their conversation. Where does your attention go? Oh yes, you heard your name all right!

In fact, you must have heard <u>all</u> of the other group's conversation or you could not have heard your name. Your subconscious, however, chose to keep the incoming information on its side of the filter because to do otherwise would have distracted your limited conscious brain from the conversation you were having. As soon as it heard your name, however, it recognised that you needed to know and it let the incoming information through the filter.

Filters, however, do more than control <u>what</u> information is allowed through to the conscious brain, they determine <u>how</u> it is allowed through.

Your filter:

- **Deletes** some information. (In the example above, it deleted the other group's conversation until your name was mentioned.)

- **Distorts** some information. (In the example above, some people might think, *'If they're saying things about me, it must be <u>criticism</u> or <u>malicious gossip</u>'* while others might think, *'I'm so popular, people are always talking about me'*.)

- **Generalises.** (And other people might think, *'People are <u>always</u> saying things about me.'*)

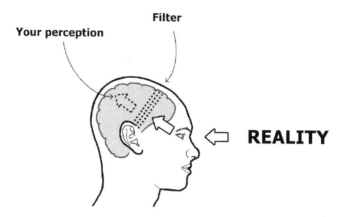

Filter
Your perception

⇦ **REALITY**

Filters can **delete, distort** and
generalise incoming information.

How filters affect confidence

People whose confidence is fragile, filter incoming information so that they do not see (delete) what they do well or claim it was luck (distort) or claim it was a one-off as they 'normally do it badly' (generalise). At a work meeting they will 'filter in' the fact that a senior manager is 'superior' to them but delete the fact that he or she is relaxed, has asked for views and that colleagues' straight-talking is being well received. When presented with an opportunity they will exaggerate (distort) the potential risk and delete the obvious benefits. Difficulty encountered in the initial stages of learning is generalised as *'I can't do it'*.

Example

A leadership course participant once asked to speak to me privately. She began by explaining that, a year ago, she had been promoted to her first team leader role. She had just received the results of the company's 360-degree appraisal process. Her manager felt she had risen to the challenge extremely well, her fellow team leaders respected her and her staff said she was the best team leader they had ever had. When I asked how I could help she replied, *'I feel like a fraud. I'm completely out of my depth as team leader'*. Then how come everyone else thought the opposite? Everyone else could see how well she had done but her filter distorted the incoming information and her paradigms made sure she felt bad about it.

Everything you 'know' about yourself, the world and your place in it is affected by some dubious programming and a very unreliable filter.

A sobering thought

Your brain won't just do this with incoming information, it will also play this trick by selecting 'evidence' from your own memories to support its programming.

Like an unscrupulous lawyer, it will suppress evidence that leads to the truth and select and distort evidence to win its case.

At times, your thinking is less of a servant to you and more of a gremlin in the machine.

FEATURE 5 - A GREMLIN IN THE MACHINE

It can come as quite a shock to realise that your brain can play tricks on you to protect its, often outdated, paradigms and programs.

Personal development involves learning and that involves reprogramming brain neurons.

Learning how to use a spreadsheet, repair a machine or complete a tax return might involve programming brain neurons but is unlikely to involve altering them in a way that contradicts paradigms or personal programs. But what about learning how to be a team leader for the first time, initiate conversations with a stranger at a social gathering or resolve conflict with a neighbour? All these learnable skills require a degree of confidence and developing that confidence may challenge paradigms (the way you think things are) and will certainly challenge personal programs (the way you think you are).

Brains don't like reprogramming that interferes with paradigms and personal programs. They resist reprogramming – even reprogramming that will benefit you.

Which raises two questions: Why do they resist? and How do they resist?

Why brains resist reprogramming

Brains resist reprogramming for three main reasons:

1. **We have a natural tendency to believe rather than doubt.** Disbelieving means putting time and effort into verifying all incoming information and possibly finding alternatives. That would take too long and, statistically, would not be necessary. So our 'default' is to believe our paradigms and programs.

2. **We have a natural tendency to associate 'causes' and 'effects' as easily as possible.** We do not have the time to investigate every event and find rational, accurate and verifiable explanations. So when, for example, incoming information about our performance contradicts our personal paradigms and programs, *'feeling like a fraud'* is a convenient way of discounting incoming information.

3. **Our brain's supreme purpose is to protect us and enable us to survive.** It can't do that if it has to constantly question its own programming.

How brains resist reprogramming

Brains have seven sneaky tricks with which they convince us that their programming is 'reality' and should be accepted without question.

Sneaky trick 1 – Cause and effect

Brains programmed for low confidence use the logic of 'cause and effect' to confirm the low-confidence programming. When something goes wrong (effect), it selects an internal cause – *'I couldn't keep up with the others'*, *'I'm no good at tight deadlines'*, *'I should have used my resources better'*. When something goes well, it selects an external cause – *'The other guys got it done despite having me on the team'*, *'The deadline was tight but, thankfully, I was lucky'*, *'The resources were poor but the task was easier than I thought it would be'*.

The internal/external choice is made subconsciously to protect existing programming.

Sneaky trick 2 - Reference groups

Brains carefully and subconsciously select reference groups (the people against whom we 'benchmark' ourselves) to support existing brain programs.

You might be comfortably well off and have more disposable income than your parents and even more than you expected when you first started work but, to confirm low confidence programming, your brain will choose reference groups more comfortably well off (or, just to add a little twist, groups that are equally well off but who have achieved that level more easily).

Brains select references that confirm their existing programs.

Sneaky trick 3 - Recognition, association and playback

The third trick by which brains convince us that their programming is reality is *recognition, association and playback.*

- **Recognition.** One of the actions at which the human brain is extremely adept is *recognition/association.* After all, in prehistoric times when meeting members of another tribe, being able to spot subtle signs of friendship or hostility was an essential skill. In the modern world, this ability is still useful - something about the salesperson's face makes us question the value of the deal being offered and we subsequently discover the item is cheaper elsewhere. Something about the way the boss is breathing makes us defer our request for time off because we realise that now is not a good time. Something about the movements of the car in front makes us give them more room just in time to prevent a collision. It is an ability that saves money, time and even lives. The problem for confidence is that, in confidence-related situations, what your brain 'recognises' has already been filtered and selected to confirm its programming.

- **Association.** The brain selects associations to reinforce its programming. When receiving incoming information, your brain cannot leave it 'pending'; it has to 'file' it. It will file it by *associating* it with existing programs even if those programs were formed in childhood, are negative, counter-productive and well past their 'use by date'.

Association is an ability that is so ingrained in us we do it without conscious intervention.

You have probably had that very common experience of hearing some music which you associate with something memorable, such as a great holiday, and memories (especially emotional memories) come flooding back.

- **Playback.** On recognising the music, however, it is rarely facts and figures that your brain associates and replays – it is *feelings*.

> *Your brain is quick to 'recognise' external stimuli*
> *and replay associated feelings.*

In confidence-challenging situations, such as a difficult presentation at work, conflict with a neighbour or talking to strangers at a party, your brain:

- **recognises** small and subtle details in the situation,

- **associates** them with 'files' and programs, many of which might easily date back to childhood,

- **replays feelings** from those earlier experiences.

As feelings have such a huge effect on behaviour in confidence-challenging situations, you have just done the equivalent of an Olympic weightlifter convincing himself that the weight he is about to try and lift is impossibly heavy. Your equivalent of the weight might be a meeting, a conversation or a request; you have psyched yourself *down* instead of psyched yourself *up*.

Sneaky trick 4 - Self-talk

> *We all have a voice inside our heads that talks to us.*
> *Unfortunately, it often psyches us down instead of up.*

How do you know if your brain is using this subtle and powerful trick? First, let's highlight something about your conscious and subconscious - the division between them is not a clear boundary; it is more of a gradual progression. Some things will be inaccessibly deep in your subconscious and others will be 'just beneath the surface', close to your conscious.

Every now and then you become consciously aware of what is going on just inside your subconscious.

One of those 'just beneath the surface' activities is *self-talk* - that little voice inside your head that talks to you. Sometimes the voice is very helpful, like a mental coach, but, often, it is critical and controlling, like a gremlin in the machine. When the voice is in gremlin mode, it tends to be emotional and critical, generalising and exaggerating to strengthen its case.

Sneaky trick 5 – Self-sabotage

Another neat trick your brain can play is to *subconsciously* direct you towards self-sabotaging behaviour.

Let's say that your brain has an *'I can't do it'* program but you also want to learn to play the piano – quite a challenge in adulthood. Your brain has several ways it can sabotage your efforts:

* **Aiming too high too soon.** Instead of starting with *Twinkle, Twinkle Little Star,* you find yourself drawn towards a Rachmaninoff concerto - a challenge even for a skilled pianist. You cannot play it and your brain's *'I can't do it'* program is safe.

* **Perfection as a reference point.** If your reference point is how you performed last month, you appreciate how much you are progressing. If your reference point is perfection, you are an obvious failure and, again, your brain's *'I can't do it'* program is safe.

* **Subtle diversion.** Learning to play the piano (and most other things you can think of) takes practice and practice takes time. If your brain convinces you that other activities are higher priority, it can sabotage your piano playing ambitions.

If your confidence is a little low, anything you want to do for yourself can easily be trumped by something you 'should' do for someone else.

Sneaky trick 6 - Comfort zones

Try this <u>as quickly as you can</u> – fold your arms. (Please don't read any further until your arms are folded.) Now look at your arms - is your right arm on top of your left arm or is your left arm on top of your right arm? You probably folded your arms the way you always do and you have been folding them so often for so many years, you did not have to think about which way to fold them. It is as if you don't even have a choice. Now fold them the other way, so that the arm that was on top is now underneath. It does not feel quite so comfortable does it?

This feeling of comfort does not just apply to the way you fold your arms; it applies to almost everything you do – your routines, your role in the family, your 'place' at work, your attitudes, values and beliefs, your self-image, your self-talk, etc, etc.

Within your comfort zone you feel ok but outside it you feel emotionally uncomfortable; the feeling of risk or potential threat gets stronger.

Your mental sat-nav setting, manifesting in your self-talk,
steers you back into your comfort zone.

Please note that a comfort zone does not have to be a pleasant place, just a familiar one. Being the family dogsbody or the office doormat are far from pleasant experiences but, for some people, they are still preferable to the relative discomfort of being something else if that something else is outside their comfort zone.

Sneaky trick 7 – Mood

As many of these sneaky tricks take place subconsciously, you are unaware of them. What you can be aware of, however, is your mood. As brains are 'wired' to give feelings priority over facts, mood controls your mental sat-nav much more effectively than rational thinking. Furthermore, as your brain feels compelled to associate an effect with a cause, if the initial trigger of a mood is not immediately obvious, it allows the filter to generalise - *everything* must be bad. Sneezes, mislaid car keys, traffic jams, uncooperative computers, delays, interruptions, etc, all feel worse when we are in a negative mood <u>and</u> they justify the mood.

SUMMARY

By now, you might be wondering why anyone would persist in allowing their brain to play all these tricks, so please remember,

- Some of them are rooted in your evolutionary past and you are not going to shake them off just because you no longer live in a cave.

- They mostly occur deep in your subconscious and, like the systems programming in a computer, it takes an expert to even know they are there, never mind access them.

It is also worth remembering that, while a lot of what your brain does is essential to your survival and daily functioning, it can also have side-effects that erode your confidence.

The purpose of this chapter, therefore, has been to show you the processes affecting your confidence.

Your brain has inherited a lot of programming from its evolutionary past and inherited paradigms and programs from parents and teachers, etc. It has a filter that fiddles with incoming information and a 'gremlin' that uses a range of sneaky tricks to keep you travelling in the direction pre-set into your internal sat-nav.

Now that you understand this, you can look at how to *make your brain work for you*.

Chapter 4

Making your brain work for you – How to *feel* confident

IS THIS YOU?

Does your own thinking sometimes sabotage your attempts to feel more confident? Do you sometimes talk yourself out of doing something your heart knows you really want to do? Do you dwell on what 'might' happen rather than on what you want to happen? Does one negative thought lead to another and, before you know what's happening, you feel 'down'? Would you like to take more control of what you think about and how you think about it?

IN THIS CHAPTER

Your subconscious brain is adept at following programs. So if you want to develop your confidence, the key is to amend the programming in your subconscious. It is essential, however, that you do this <u>the easy way</u> rather than by trying to exert Herculean amounts of willpower.

Whether or not you feel confident is a function of the way you think or, more precisely, the way your brain has been programmed to think. The easy way to change that programming is to tag new instructions onto existing programs and make them work for you.

FIVE IMPORTANT CONCEPTS

Here are the five most important concepts that form the key to tagging new instructions onto existing programs.

Concept 1 - Your brain is 'plastic'

'Plasticity' is the term neuroscientists use to refer to the brain's ability to be reprogrammed. At one time they thought it was only 'plastic' in childhood and became 'fixed' in adulthood. Now neuroscientists believe that many aspects of the brain remain plastic even into adulthood. This means that the way you think can be changed.

Concept 2 - Firing thresholds can be high or low

Brain neurons have multiple, branching structures called dendrites. Dendrites have 'terminals' for transmitting and receiving nerve impulses and forming 'contacts' with the terminals of other dendrites. Masses of dendrites interlink in different combinations by sending impulses across the synapses (the tiny gaps between dendrites) from one combination to another. A combination of neurons firing together is what I refer to, loosely, as a program.

When a program is well established, the resultant actions or thoughts feel easy, comfortable and normal because the firing threshold is low. It does not take much to trigger it. Conversely, when a program is new to us, the firing threshold is high and the resultant actions or thoughts feel difficult, uncomfortable and strange. That feeling (difficult, uncomfortable, strange) is a normal part of the learning (reprogramming) process. That is why learning requires repetition.

Repetition is the important part; it just happens to take time. It is a bit like cutting back vegetation to make a path through jungle. If the journey is only made once or twice, the vegetation quickly regrows and the path is lost. If the new path is walked repeatedly over only a few weeks, it quickly becomes established.

Concept 3 - Perception is your 'reality'

Brains can be very selective. They protect their programming by carefully selecting 'evidence' from reference groups and memory associations. In fact, everything you know, believe, and feel about yourself, other people and the world around you has been filtered by your subconscious. So, you don't have to change actual reality, only the way you filter information - that automatically changes your 'perceived reality'.

Concept 4 - Perception changes as position changes

Perceptual Position is a very useful concept that will help you understand, and subsequently take more control of, your thinking.

As a reminder, incoming information is filtered according to our paradigms and programs. This means that, as everyone's experiences are individual, our perceptions are individual (see diagram below).

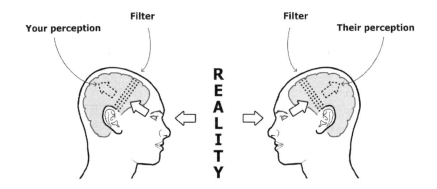

You might have heard the saying *the map is not the territory.* It can't be; it can only ever be a *representation* of reality – the roads, rivers and railways on a map are *representations* of the real roads, rivers and railways. Some maps are accurate and up to date and others are old and have been outdated by new roads, etc. The map you use, therefore, could be different from the map someone else is using. It is the same with perception.

Concept 5 - Feelings aren't facts

Imagine if someone who has been taking sugar in coffee decides to give it up. Initially, the sugarless coffee tastes awful but, after a couple of weeks, it tastes normal; it is coffee *with* sugar that now tastes awful.

In actual *fact*, coffee with, and coffee without sugar taste the same as they always did – it is the person's *feeling* about the taste that has changed. It is a *fact* that the coffee has no sugar; it is *feeling* that the person did not like it. Two weeks later it is still *fact* that it has no sugar; it is *feeling* that the person now enjoys it.

Being aware of feelings, yours and other people's, is helpful; interpreting them as if they were facts is not.

It's your brain so let's make it work for you. Let's see how you can use these concepts to **feel more confident**. (We will look at behaving more confidently in the next chapter.) Here is a range of tips that will help you.

SWITCH YOUR REFERENCE POINT

Broadly, your mental reference point can be in one of two places, *internal* or *external*. Each place has advantages and disadvantages.

- An **internal reference point** can help you stand up for what you believe is right. This is essential when your opinion is in the minority and you need the courage of your convictions or you need to resist peer pressure.

- An **external reference point** can help you make sacrifices for the greater good, persevere through problems to achieve a long term goal or critically examine your own perspective by comparing it to other people's.

When your confidence is low, however, an internal reference point can become a handicap by making you focus on your own negative feelings. Standing up for yourself takes you out of your comfort zone and makes you feel uncomfortable, so you give in. It can also make you focus on your own outdated paradigms; putting yourself first, for example, even only occasionally, feels selfish. An external reference point makes you more aware of other people's rights than of your own rights, it makes majority views difficult to resist, despite your own convictions, and it makes you susceptible to peer pressure.

The 'trick' is to realise that:

- You already use these two broad reference points.

- You can **choose which one you use** and **when you use it**; you can switch between them and use the one that leads you towards the best outcome in any given situation.

How do you know which is the right one at any moment? Ask yourself, are you trying to avoid short-term, emotional discomfort knowing that it will result in a longer-term problem? If so, you probably need to switch your reference point.

Use the reference point that leads you <u>towards</u> the best outcome.

REDIRECT YOUR MOTIVATION

While we can be motivated by many things, the *direction* of our motivation in relation to any specific issue usually points in one of two directions:

- **Towards** something we want.

- **Away from** something we don't want.

There are advantages and disadvantages to both motivational directions.

Away from motivation can be very effective in avoiding problems or even physical harm. Don't play with fire, you can get burned. Don't skimp on your course work, you'll get poor grades. *Away from* motivation can be very efficient. Its efficiency, however, is very situation-specific; when *away from* motivation becomes a habit we suffer three problems:

- First, moving *away from* what you <u>do not</u> want does not necessarily take you closer to what you <u>do</u> want. It is like a sat-nav that gives directions to avoid congestion but does not have a destination; any destination will do as long as it is 'not here'.

- Second, brains are not very good at processing negatives. See if, <u>for the next five seconds</u>, you can fulfil the following instruction – *'Do <u>not</u> think about elephants'*..........Ok, five seconds is up. How did you do? I bet as soon as you read the word 'elephant' you thought of one and then you had to *deliberately* think about something else. That is a major problem of *away from* instructions – the brain has two steps to process. Step one, *'Do not think about that'*. Step two, *'Think about this instead'*. Wouldn't it be more efficient to go straight to the positive instruction?

- Third, the farther away you get from whatever it is you want to avoid, the less it motivates. Think about it - if you are running away from a hazard, the greater the distance between you and the hazard, the sooner you can slow down. Applied to an emergency, that might be sufficient but, for most other situations, the key point about *away from* motivation is that, when you stop running, your location may not be a good one.

Not being where you don't want to be is not the same as being where you do want to be.

Towards motivation, on the other hand, has lots of advantages:

- It is very specific. 'If you do your coursework well, you'll get the grades you need and get to your first choice college'. 'If you stand your ground on this issue, people will be more inclined to take you seriously from now on.'

- It talks the brain's language – none of the confusing negatives that the brain has difficulty processing.

- Just like approaching the finishing line in a race, the closer you get to what you want, the stronger its motivational effect on your behaviour.

Focus on what you want and make your description of it as detailed, precise and attractive as possible.

USE PERCEPTUAL POSITIONING WHEN REFLECTING ON A NEGATIVE EXPERIENCE

Perception is how you see, understand or interpret something. A *perceptual position*, therefore, is how you see, understand or interpret something (perceive it) from where you are, your role or your experience (your position).

You have probably had the experience of being in dialogue with someone and realising that how you perceive the situation is different from how they perceive it. So, in a conversation between you and one other person, how many perceptual positions are there? Two? Yours and theirs? No, there are three – yours, theirs and that of *an imaginary independent observer* (see diagram below).

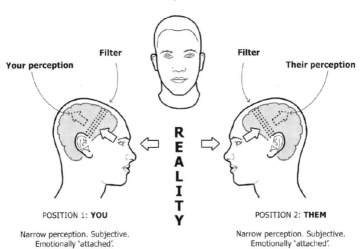

POSITION 3: **INDEPENDENT OBSERVER**

Wide perception. Objective.
Emotionally 'detached'.

Filter   Filter

Your perception   Their perception

R
E
A
L
I
T
Y

POSITION 1: **YOU**   POSITION 2: **THEM**

Narrow perception. Subjective.   Narrow perception. Subjective.
Emotionally 'attached'.   Emotionally 'attached'.

The problem with position 1 (you) and position 2 (the other person) is that the field of vision is narrow and, hence, limited. Perception is easily affected by paradigms and often by the emotions your brain associates with the situation. This makes it difficult to see the situation objectively.

The benefit of position 3 is that independent observers are usually much better placed to understand all viewpoints, be emotionally detached and, consequently, be more objective. By way of example, you will have experienced position 3 any time you have listened to a friend complain about someone else and, because of your emotional detachment, you could see both sides of the argument and, consequently, a way of resolving the problem. Skilled arbitrators regularly use position 3.

You can deliberately move between perceptual positions.

Moving between perceptual positions has real benefits

Negative experiences, whether real or replayed in your imagination, generate negative emotions but, if you never reflect on such experiences, you will never learn anything of value from them. Ask yourself this question, how much do you learn when you replay them from position 1? Not much. In fact, you probably reinforce unhelpful programs confirming that you are bad at handling such conversations or that 'people like that' really annoy you. This does not help your confidence. You can probably see yourself going backwards along the spiral!

Imagine if, instead, you replayed negative experiences from position 3 which, as you know, is more emotionally detached, objective and solution orientated. Replaying a conversation from position 3 is easier when you imagine you are watching the conversation on a screen such as your television, laptop or tablet. Use your imagination to speak with a calm, positive voice, to change your body language and to change the words you speak.

In conversations where emotions are running high, for example, people exaggerate (*'You're always doing...'*), generalise (*'This is typical of people like you'*) or use sarcasm (*'I know this is asking a lot of your one remaining brain cell but...'*). From your imaginary position 3, you can 'translate' the other person's words making them more specific and rational (*'That report wasn't in the format I asked for. I'd like to run through it again, see why there was a misunderstanding and agree how it can be rewritten within the deadline'.*)

You will notice that observing the conversation from position 3, even within your own imagination, enables you to a) stay in control of your emotions, b) appreciate the other person's perception and c) identify valuable advice for the person in position 1 (you). In other words, you learn something helpful from the process of reflection.

As you practise 'position 3 thinking', you will quickly develop the ability to reflect on a situation objectively and incisively. In doing so, you will automatically change the firing threshold of your response to other people's negative behaviours and you will find it increasingly easy to remain calm. You will also see how to handle the situation better next time. The quality of your reflection and preparation both improve.

Remember, it is your imagination - you can make it work for you.

USE PERCEPTUAL POSITIONING WHEN PREPARING FOR A CHALLENGING SITUATION

You can also use perceptual position 3 when preparing for a challenging situation. Turn on your imaginary television and tell the actors 'action'. As the scriptwriter, producer and director, you instruct them what to say and how to say it. You can make yourself confident and assertive and you can make the other person as much of a challenge as you want. You can get the actors to do as many 'takes' as you like until the actor in position 1 (you) has got it right (it's your imagination, remember). Then, when the actor in position 1 has got it exactly right, you can 'morph' into position 1 yourself and rehearse it a few more times, seeing the scene not on an imaginary screen but as if through your own eyes.

Perceptual positioning really is a versatile tool, so move into the perceptual position that boosts your confidence whenever you need to.

USE PERCEPTUAL POSITIONING WHEN REFLECTING ON A GOOD EXPERIENCE

In the same way that replaying a negative experience from position 1 will make you feel bad, replaying a positive experience from position 1 will make you feel good.

Just as people will replay a movie or piece of music to trigger the good feelings they associate with it, you can do the same with good experiences. Someone's kind remark, someone's genuine thanks, some praise at work, a baby's laugh, a beautiful sunset, a winning goal, fun with friends, etc, all become *'resources' you can tap into any time you need a confidence boost.* (You might even be thinking of more personal experiences right now.)

When you replay good experiences from position 1, you top up your confidence so that it will be fully charged whenever you need it.

REFRAME

Another versatile tool is reframing.

Just as changing the frame around a picture can transform the way you feel about it, changing the way you 'frame' (that is, *perceive*) a situation affects how you filter it, feel about it and behave in it.

Reframing changes expectation, motivation and self-talk.

Examples

Playing a sport such as tennis against someone better than you can be 'framed' as a hopeless task or as an opportunity to learn in real time. A broken television can be 'framed' as a boring evening or as an opportunity to rediscover the art of conversation or the pleasure of being 'lost' in a good book. Losing a job can be 'framed' as uncomfortable insecurity or as an opportunity to make some fundamental life-changing decisions. It all depends on how you *choose* to perceive it – how you choose to frame it.

Reframing works so well because:

- As your brain is wired to give emotional thoughts priority over rational thoughts, you avoid becoming tangled in a struggle between negative feelings and rational thoughts; you simply change the negative feeling for a more positive one and hitch a ride on it.

- Second, your brain cannot leave a thought isolated; it has to *associate* it with paradigms, memories and self-talk. Reframing triggers helpful associations, moving you forwards along the spiral.

Difficult people and challenging situations provide fertile ground for reframing. The stubborn person becomes an opportunity to test your persuasive skills. The person who puts you down is presenting situations in which you can practise some of the assertive skills we will look at in the next chapter. Potential conflict with someone becomes an opportunity to understand each other better and improve the relationship.

Reframing is great for changing the way you see challenging situations.

USE POSITIVE WORDS

Closely linked to framing and perceptual positions are the words you use in both your self-talk and when you talk to other people.

In this context, words have a twofold purpose.

- They provide a big clue about your underlying *state* (how you feel in relation to a forthcoming activity).

- They are also one of the means by which you can alter your state.

Examples

'I've got to go to Tom's leaving party' or *'I really should go to Tom's leaving party'*. The words 'got to' and 'should' imply you are being compelled to go to Tom's party against your will. On that premise, it is unlikely you will enjoy it. On the other hand, if you think, *'I'll go to Tom's leaving party so that he knows I wish him well in his new job,'* this indicates that you are choosing to go.

'I should stand up for myself more but I can't do it.' There is that word 'should' again but now we have added the ultimate 'get-out' because if you really can't do it, there is no point trying. So, not only can you now confirm your low confidence, you can also feel bad because in addition to being unable to do it, it is something you *should* do - a negative double-whammy. On the other hand, if you think, *'I'm learning to stand up for myself'* or *'I can't do it yet'* you are putting yourself into a much more positive and resourceful state.

'Yet' is far more than a word, it is a state of mind.
Your expectation is clear.

While we all use negative words sometimes - it is the pattern and the consistency that are important because, when words are positive, the pattern and consistency make the thinking/behaviour spiral work in your favour.

Whether speaking to yourself or to other people, use words that are accurate, objective and solution-orientated. They are far more confidence-building for you and far more uplifting for those around you.

CONSIDER YOUR RIGHTS AS WELL AS YOUR RESPONSIBILITIES

You are probably already used to the fact that you have rights. Some are enshrined in law and some are defined by contract. But what about the common sense rights to which confident people feel they are entitled? Do you, for example, believe you have a right to:

- Be listened to?

- Be taken seriously?

- Have, and express, an opinion?

- Ask for help, assistance and cooperation?

- Say 'No' when it is appropriate?

- Put yourself first occasionally?

- Choose your mood; choose how you feel?

This is an illustrative list; you can probably think of many more. One of the key points about rights is that they make it easier to behave confidently.

Example

You are in a meeting at work attended by some colleagues who can be quite forceful. You are trying to make a point that you feel is important but one of the attendees keeps interrupting you. When you accept your right to be listened to, it becomes easier to assert yourself and say something like, *'Just a minute, please, Bill. Let me finish my point and then I'll be able to listen to yours.'* You finish your point and another attendee belittles your point with some sarcasm. If you accept your right to be taken seriously, it is easier to respond with something like, *'Jean, be fair. My point deserves consideration. If you have a specific comment, I'm happy to listen to it'.*

Balance rights with responsibilities

When people become over-confident, even arrogant, they grab lots of rights for themselves and ignore other people's rights. When people feel low confidence, they accept other people's rights but not their own. Neither approach is fair or balanced.

When you have the right level of confidence, however, you balance every right with a corresponding responsibility. That way, you will always be fair to yourself and to other people. If you want the right to be listened to, for example, you accept the responsibility to listen to others - even if they contaminate their point with sarcasm. If you want the right to choose your own feelings, you accept the responsibility to stay calm when someone else allows their emotions to affect what they say.

Consider your rights and corresponding responsibilities from position 3 and let them guide your behaviour.

ASK THE RIGHT QUESTION

The power of questions

While some questions are undoubtedly genuine, some questions can be manipulative because they contain an underlying assumption. Market researchers, for example, have long known that if they ask people, *'How happy are you with your life?'* answers skew towards optimism but when they ask, *'How unhappy are you with your life?* answers skew towards pessimism.

Prompted by the question, different associations
are triggered in the brain.

Questions trigger associations.

Example

When your confidence is a bit low and you are fumbling over flat-pack furniture, frustration escalates and you ask yourself, *'Why can't I do this?'* The association is triggered and your subconscious <u>obediently finds the answer</u> – *'Because you're useless'*. Just imagine if you asked a different question such as, *'How can I do this more easily?'* or *'What do I need to do to get this done simply?'* Again your subconscious <u>obediently finds the answer</u> and tells you to *'Read the instructions more slowly'* or *'Ask someone to hold the pieces while you screw them together'*.

There is another reason for asking the right question and engaging in positive self-talk. As your filtering process is so effective, brains more easily see what they expect to see rather than what is actually there. So your brain will notice 'evidence' that supports the associations triggered by the seemingly innocent question or comment.

Questions trigger associations. So always ask yourself the
right question – one that is positive and empowering.

CONVERT YOUR BRAIN'S GREMLIN INTO A MENTAL MENTOR

We all have a voice inside our head that talks to us – an *inner voice*. Sometimes, unfortunately, its purpose is to communicate and reinforce paradigms and programs that don't help us. When you listen to it objectively and analyse it, you will discover that what it says is often dominated by 'parental' language.

When parents speak to children, a lot of what they say communicates and reinforces rules. They tell children what they *must/must not, should/should not, ought/ought not* and *can/ cannot do.*

> *It is often this controlling and disempowering style that your inner voice adopts as it communicates and reinforces your subconscious programs.*

Also, as the purpose of your inner voice is to save you from harm and hassle, it will err on the side of caution, exaggerating risk or telling you that you are unable to do something – even when the risk is tiny or you could probably learn to do it.

The result is that, too often, you are subconsciously dissuaded from doing something - from speaking up, from standing your ground, from negotiating a fair way forward, from standing up for your rights, from enjoying yourself, from being adventurous and so on. <u>This reinforces low confidence.</u>

> *When you intervene in your self-talk, you can change <u>what</u> it says and <u>how</u> it says it, converting it from a sabotaging gremlin into a mental mentor.*

But (and this is a big 'but'), as most self-talk is subconscious, we need to ask, 'How do you change it if you are not consciously aware of it'?

How to make positive self-talk a habit

Step 1 - Pay conscious attention to your mood. If your mood is positive, it is almost certainly because your self-talk is positive. If your mood is negative, it is almost certainly because your self-talk is negative.

Step 2 - Increase the frequency with which you pay conscious attention to your mood. This is important. You are probably using the limited capacity of your conscious brain to do things that require conscious thought – answer emails, shop, cross the road safely and so on. Your self-talk will chatter away subconsciously and, before you know it, you are feeling negative. By then, you have a big task to change the direction of your thoughts and feelings. So increasing the frequency with which you check your mood can mean smaller and easier changes of direction.

Step 3 - Use external stimuli as a trigger to check your mood. The external stimuli can be anything that enters your conscious – a police siren, the sound of an aircraft, a squeaking door, someone else's conversation, a ringing telephone, birdsong, the breeze rustling leaves, a need to stretch or yawn. Anything. Like all habits, it can take a little time to develop this stimulus/response association but, after a while, it feels natural and automatic.

Step 4 - Move into position 3 and change your self-talk. Make it specific (rather than general), descriptive (rather than judgemental) and solution orientated (rather than disempowering).

Help your self-talk work for you as a mental coach,
guide and mentor.

CHANGE YOUR 'STATE'

State is how you feel, your mood. You are probably already good at changing your state without realising it. For example, you probably enjoy a party more when you get yourself into a party state. You probably perform better at sport when you get yourself into an energetic or competitive state. You probably enjoy a better night's sleep when you get yourself into a relaxed, peaceful state. These are three common examples of improving your 'performance' (at enjoying yourself, playing sport and sleeping) by changing your state for a specific situation.

If you are wondering whether you can follow the same principle when you need to 'perform' confidently, the answer is a loud and resounding 'yes' and the method is simple!

Three things seem to be inextricably linked – your breathing, your posture and your state. So:

- breathe more slowly and deeply, with even control of the inhale and the exhale,

- stand more upright, raise your gaze, walk a bit faster,

- smile at the person you pass or for whom you hold open a door; deliberately notice good things – a helpful person, a happy child, a splendid tree or a beautiful flower.

Within two or three minutes you will feel brighter, more optimistic and more empowered. You will have changed your state in three minutes and that's a promise. What's more, as you develop this simple skill, you will get better and faster at it.

You have the right to choose how you feel. Use that right and your mood becomes a springboard to confident action.

RESET YOUR MOOD THERMOSTAT

You are probably familiar with thermostats that control room temperature. You set the thermostat to a temperature at which you feel comfortable and, as the temperature rises, the thermostat triggers the air conditioning. As the temperature drops, the thermostat triggers the heating. In this way, the temperature remains within a set range; a level you feel is normal. But what would happen if each day you changed the thermostat a tiny fraction? How long would it take before the new temperature became the new 'normal'?

Something similar can happen to us when we allow negative thoughts to affect us over a period of only a few days or weeks. Our new, negative mood feels normal. Then the brain does its stuff and we seek associations and use our filter to *confirm* the new mood as normal. You have, without realising, reset your mood thermostat.

Why not reset your mood thermostat deliberately? Combine as many tips as possible. Move the thermostat a fraction each day. Expect each new 'temperature' to feel a little odd. It might take hours, days or even a couple of weeks, depending on the degree of change, but it *will* change. That is a certainty.

Decide on the new 'normal' and use a combination of tips to reset your mood thermostat a small amount each day.

MANAGE THE MESSAGES FROM YOUR ENVIRONMENT

We know that the brain filters in what it expects to see and filters out what is not congruent with its expectations. This raises a question – what makes the brain expect to see certain things and not others? The main expectations will stem from paradigms, programs and even moods. You can, however, stimulate the process of changing expectations by changing the messages that come from your environment.

By way of example, people tend to manage their working time better and feel less stressed when their working environment is tidy. Some people feel better about themselves when they buy new clothes. Some people like their home more when they de-clutter.

We humans are very susceptible to the messages we receive from our environment.

So, if you want to feel better about your body, stop reading 'celebrity magazines' full of beautiful people with nothing better to do all day than preen themselves, wear designer clothes and pose for staged photographs that are then airbrushed to perfection. If you want to feel upbeat at coffee breaks, don't join the group who spend fifteen minutes wallowing in the state of the economy, the questionable integrity of some politicians or how the weather wrecked their weekend.

Instead read factual newspapers, watch television programmes that entertain or inform you and mix with people who invigorate you. It won't be long before you are invigorating them.

Nurture your mind and your mood follows.

REVIEW AND PREVIEW

Feeling confident will probably mean changing some of your brain's programming. Thankfully, that is easier when you realise that your brain is 'plastic' and that repetition is the key to changing even those programs that have high firing thresholds. Repeated use of simple techniques is all it takes.

In this chapter we have looked at those techniques - changing perceptual positions, redirecting your motivation, reframing the way you perceive situations, using positive words, balancing your rights and responsibilities, asking yourself the right questions, turning your gremlin into a mentor, changing your state, resetting your mood thermostat and managing the messages from your environment so that they feed your growing confidence.

Whether you use all or only a selection of these suggestions, you will feel more confident; they intervene in the processes your brain performs naturally and, with a few small changes, make those processes work for you.

You can build on this foundation of confident thinking by using the tips in the next chapter so that you also behave confidently.

Chapter 5

Making your behaviour work for you – How to *behave* confidently

IS THIS YOU?

How often does your body language show that you lack confidence? How often does your confidence desert you at the crucial moment? To what extent do you avoid situations in which you might have to meet new people or engage in small talk? Do you sometimes feel unable to ask for what you want, respond to a put-down, stand your ground, say 'No' or disagree with someone? Do you sometimes 'lose it' when something takes you by surprise? Would you like your behaviour to be confident more often?

IN THIS CHAPTER

In the same way that the previous chapter showed you how to *think* confidently, this chapter shows you how to *behave* confidently.

Some of the tips are deceptively simple and others are slightly more detailed. So feel free to start where you feel most comfortable.

When you feel confident, it is easier to behave more confidently; when you behave more confidently, it is easier to feel more confident.

We'll begin with a few important concepts to ensure we're on the same wavelength.

IMPORTANT CONCEPTS

New behaviour can feel strange at first

That is normal. New *anything* can feel strange at first. New shoes, a new hobby or a new job all feel strange until you get used to them and personalise them. Some people, when initially behaving confidently, feel as if they are 'faking' it. That is only one way of framing new behaviour. Frame it another way and you will feel as if you are learning, developing, progressing along the spiral, etc. It's your choice, so why not choose positively?

Constant communication

We human beings are constantly communicating.

All behaviour communicates something and all communication achieves something.

When you avoid eye contact, wag a finger at someone, wring your hands or fidget, you communicate something. Even how you breathe communicates something. (Have you ever asked someone to do something and their immediate response is to sigh? Doesn't that communicate a lot?)

Even when you are on your own you are still communicating - your subconscious is listening! Our brains and bodies feed back to each other; a drawn out sigh as you see that there is nothing interesting on television or an impatient huff as the computer takes too long to do something is picked up by your own brain, filtered and associated with corresponding paradigms. Having allowed in the thin end of the wedge, you feel even more disappointed or impatient.

So it makes sense to control the messages you transmit to others and the messages you transmit to yourself - especially as the *meaning* of what you communicate is your responsibility.

The meaning of communication

When you consider that everything you communicate has to pass through the recipient's filter where it might be deleted, distorted or generalised, you are leaving a lot to chance if you relinquish responsibility for clear communication to the recipient. It is far safer to assume that you are responsible for the *received meaning* of what you communicate and communicate clearly and precisely no matter what situation you are in.

Situation-specific communication

Communication does not exist in a vacuum; its *received meaning* is affected by the situation. (For example, if you jump to your feet in a library and start screaming, everyone will look at you in stunned silence. Do the same on board an aircraft and other passengers will start screaming too. Same behaviour, different situation, so different received meaning and, consequently, different response.) Similarly, using the broken record (which will be explained shortly) to say *'No'* to an unreasonable request from a manipulative colleague might be sensible; using the broken record to say *'No'* to a reasonable request from your manager the day before your performance review might be career suicide.

All of these tips will serve you better when you apply some situation-specific common sense. However, because of your paradigms, programs and filters, please make sure you apply *objective, 'position 3' common sense*, rather than 'common sense' filtered through position 1 emotion. It also helps when you focus on your enduring confidence-building goals, rather than on a momentary mood.

Now for the tips. You are welcome to read them in sequence or to skim through them and find answers to your most pressing issues.

A GOOD PLACE TO START

Here are four simple tips that have a disproportionately big effect.

1 Smile

Smiling is good. Not only, in most situations, do other people like it when you smile and assume you are confident, smiling releases feel-good endorphins in your brain. Furthermore, because of the feedback mechanisms between brain and body, you feel better. So it is worth asking whether your default facial expression is a smile or frown. Do you tend to look happy, sad, anxious, impatient or what? Think about the old saying - *by the time you're fifty you get the face you deserve.* So why not make it a happy, attractive and confident face? (By the way, if you are over fifty years of age, smiling is effective 'rectification' work.)

2 Walk with purpose

When you feel a lack of confidence or when your mood is 'down', your walk tends to feel more 'leaden', less buoyant, less purposeful. When you walk with pace and purpose, you look and feel better and, because of the brain/body feedback mechanisms, your 'state' improves.

3 Make eye contact

Eye contact (along with a smile) is one of the first things to disappear when people lack confidence. So the next time you walk into a meeting, enter a dentist's waiting room or hold open a door for someone, smile and make eye contact. Not only will most people reciprocate, which is nice, but by practising in these easy situations, smiling and eye contact will quickly become a habit for you. This means that they will come more easily to you in challenging situations - which is precisely when you need them.

Eye contact is also an important part of our communication when we want to add gravity, sincerity or confidence to what we say. So, if eye contact does not come naturally to you yet, especially in challenging situations, it is worth practising. You can begin by looking at the other person's lips or at the bridge of their nose. This is relatively easy and, at normal business and social distance, looks just like eye contact. It is also useful practice to hold eye contact for slightly longer than you normally would.

4 Sit and stand like a newsreader

A newsreader's posture has four main characteristics:

- They sit or stand upright. This helps them breathe slowly and deeply which is very relaxing.

- The deep breathing means that, as they speak, they can gently push slightly more air over their vocal cords. This makes their voice sound slightly deeper, more resonant and better projected.

- By looking at the camera they appear to be making eye contact directly with us.

- Their hands are usually on display, loosely clasped in front of them.

This overall combination makes newsreaders appear relaxed, confident and authoritative. It will do the same for you and, thanks to your brain/body feedback, it will make you *feel* relaxed, confident and authoritative too.

> *When you control your breathing and posture,*
> *you control your 'state'.*

When you get into the right state, you do more than feel and look more confident; your brain is more susceptible to positive associations, positive performance and positive programming.

So the next time you are in a meeting, at a desk or even at the kitchen table and want to be taken seriously, gently ease into newsreader posture. You too will appear confident and authoritative and your brain, picking up these cues, will start associating and accessing confident programs.

TRY MODELLING

Modelling produces very quick results. You have probably already done it without realising.

Example 1 - Riding a bike and Catch 22

Can you ride a bicycle? If you can, there was probably a time when you could not – you could only ride a tricycle or a bike with stabilizers. One day, someone you trusted suggested trying a bicycle without stabilizers. If you had then tried to ride the bike unaided, your gremlin would probably have made you go slowly so that, if you lost your balance, you could safely put down a foot and avoid falling off. (Your gremlin, remember, wants to keep you safe.) In this situation, its attempt to keep you safe puts you in a 'Catch 22' situation – you cannot ride a bicycle so your gremlin gets you to ride very slowly; riding a bicycle very slowly is difficult even for experienced cyclists so, for a novice, it is virtually impossible. That is the catch; failure is guaranteed. Your gremlin breathes a sigh of relief; its *'I can't ride a bike'* program prevails.

To counteract this problem, the trusted person offers to hold the back of the bike while you pedal. As you build up speed you check that he or she is still holding the bike and keeping you safe. Eventually you realise that the trusted person is just running behind you and no longer supporting you but, by now, you are going too fast to put down a foot. You have been capable of riding a bike ever since!

The key point in relation to modelling is that you probably rode perfectly for quite some distance just because you *thought* someone had hold of the bike. In other words, *you were physically capable of riding the bike; the only thing stopping you was your mental gremlin.* The trusted person effectively tricked your gremlin *into letting you do what you were capable of doing.*

Does this work in adulthood? Oh yes!

Example 2 - The job interview

Imagine going for an interview for a job or promotion you really, really want. Your gremlin wants to save you from disappointment and it wants to preserve any programs relating to your ability, role, place in the world, etc. So it causes you to imagine, from position 1, a stressful interview, it uses negative self-talk to get you into a poor state and, as you walk into the interview room, it triggers your fight or flight response so that the interviewers get a weak, sweaty, 'wet fish' handshake from you.

Now imagine going for a job interview just to get some interview practice. It's a great job but they want someone better qualified or more experienced. The only reason for going is that the interview will be good experience for when another job comes up; this one is a no-hoper. So you relax. Your gremlin has nothing to worry about *so it lets you do the interview unhindered.* The interviewers like you so much they offer you the job. Does this sound far-fetched? I find that, when I ask people if they have ever attended an interview just for practice, a big majority of those who have done so were (much to their surprise) offered the job. A big majority. Why?

> *You can do quite a lot when you bypass your*
> *'I can't do it' program.*

Bypass your 'I can't do it' program

In fact, we are often very capable people when we bypass the feelings and self-talk that would hold us back. That is the essence of modelling – it enables you to bypass your gremlin. The simplest and easiest trick is to *pretend*. (You were probably really good at pretending when you were a child so I am sure you can rekindle the skill.) You pretend to be confident, to be tolerant, to be a good listener – whatever it is that will make it easier for your latent skills to come to the fore.

Modelling can be used *specifically* and *generally*.

Specific modelling

Imagine you are in a work meeting with very senior managers. You have just delivered a presentation. Your goal is for them to approve your recommendations but, first, they are going to interrogate you. You know that they are more likely to accept your recommendations if they feel that you are confident in your answers. While you are, indeed, confident in your recommendations, you can feel the nerves starting to rise and you know that, if you appear nervous, the senior managers may reject your proposal.

Who do you know who comes across confidently? It might be someone in another department, a politician or a television news reader. Whoever it is, use them as your model and pretend to be them. Do not try to mimic their voice or accent; just pretend to have their relaxed emotions, their upright posture, their comfortable breathing, their calm and reassuring voice, their inclusive eye contact, and so on. (If you have a fertile imagination, you can even pretend that they have taken over your body - a bit like the way Patrick Swayze took over Whoopi Goldberg's body in the movie *Ghost*. It still looked and sounded like Whoopi Goldberg but she communicated in the calm confident manner of Patrick Swayze.) When you 'model' someone, it still looks and sounds like you but the feelings, emotions and confidence are theirs.

Whether the situation is a meeting at work, a tricky conversation about a neighbour's behaviour or a discussion about rights and responsibilities in the family, modelling makes it easier for you to talk so that people find it easier to listen to you and take you seriously. It also makes it easier for you to stay calm and listen genuinely to them. That is a pretty good combination.

General modelling

You can also use modelling generally. One of the 'negative spiral' effects of a lack of confidence is *procrastination* – that inertia-hugging tendency to put things off. Your gremlin does, of course, ensure that you have a 'valid' reason for putting things off. It combines assessment of risk, reference groups, motivational direction, comfort zones and anything else it can use to convince you that you should do nothing – *it will take too long, it won't be worth it, it will be too difficult, now is not a good time, you're not sure if you'll like it, it's too much trouble, etc, etc.* The pay-off is the momentary relief of avoiding whatever it is that your gremlin doesn't want you to do but the cost is a big one – cumulative dissatisfaction with yourself.

Modelling helps in these situations too. All you do, when you feel procrastination creeping up on you is to ask, 'What would a confident person do in this situation?' and then, pretend to be confident enough to take *the first step.* It might be as simple as finding a telephone number, sending an email or booking a ticket. That is both the irony of procrastination and the trick in switching it off - the first step is the most difficult, yet it is often incredibly simple. Once you have made that step, the journey has begun.

Good ideas only have to work some of the time to get you closer to the outcome you want more of the time.

Getting closer means that, when you reflect on the situation, you see the difference in your emotions and behaviour. This moves you along the spiral in the right direction and knowing that you are moving along the spiral in the right direction reinforces your confidence and all you have done is a few seconds (literally) of pretending. Simple!

MAKE SMALL TALK

Talking to strangers in social situations is something that some people find so uncomfortable they will avoid such situations as much as possible. If they can't avoid them, they stand on their own or latch onto someone and frequently dry up in conversations.

When you think about it, small talk should be easy (that's why it's called 'small talk'). So something must be getting in the way. As usual, that 'something' will be a combination of thinking and behaviour so here is a range of ideas that will help you work on both:

- **Check and correct your self-talk** from position 3.

- **Reframe the situation.** It might be a great opportunity to meet new and interesting people, hear fresh views on things, practise confident behaviours such as eye contact and relaxed newsreader posture, get some free food and drink, etc.

- As you walk in, **model someone** you know or have seen who is good at these situations. You will probably find that you will walk in purposefully, your posture will be newsreader upright, you will have a friendly smile and good eye contact. If you see someone you know, go and join them. If you don't see anyone you know, get a coffee, glass of wine or whatever is available and then join someone. Anyone standing by themselves will likely welcome your approach. Alternatively, approach a small group, smile, make eye contact, say 'Hello', tell them your name and ask if you can join them. (Remember, they were probably all strangers 30 seconds before you joined them.) Acting *as if* you are pleased to meet people automatically creates a natural smile and eye contact.

- Now that you have someone to talk to – **listen.** The best way of listening is to trigger their talking with a short question or statement. *'I've walked by this building so many times and* *always wondered what it's like on the inside. Isn't it wonderful?'* or *'I wasn't expecting so many people. Isn't it a really good turn out?'* Their answer will probably lead to another easy question, *'Have you had chance for a look round yet?'* or *'How do you know the host'?*

- As the conversation progresses, you can **introduce new, easy and 'safe' questions** about, for example, the weather, a popular television programme, a news headline or the other person's job. (The more you absorb information from the news, current affairs etc, the more subjects you will be able to introduce or contribute.)

- You can also **contribute relevant information** about yourself. As people talk about their jobs, hobbies, holidays etc, you can reciprocate (but keep detail in reserve to respond to their questions). A little 'me too' reciprocity facilitates small talk.

Two issues that make some people wary of these social situations are remembering people's names and getting 'stuck' with someone.

- The easiest way to embed anything in your memory is repetition so, as you hear someone's name, repeat it in your imagination while looking at their face as they are answering your question (see above). If you have just been introduced to several people, repeat their names *in sequence* several times, in your imagination. Do that again every ten to twenty seconds and you will be pleasantly surprised how quickly their names stick.

- Helping people's names stick in your memory is good. Being 'stuck' with someone isn't. The simplest strategy to detach yourself from someone is to suggest you both join another group's conversation or that it has been a pleasure chatting to them and now you need to mingle.

When you approach social gatherings this way, you benefit from real-time practice of modelling, eye contact, etc, you enlarge your comfort zone and you enjoy the company of interesting people.

The sooner you meet new people, the sooner
you have old friends.

MAKE A REQUEST

Some conversation openings, like *'How was your weekend?'* are easy. Other conversation openings like *'I need you to work late tonight'* are more difficult. When we have to make a request *and* lack confidence, we tend to make three mistakes:

- We procrastinate and defer the request until the very last moment by when the issue is more critical or inconvenient.

- We beat about the bush in a subconscious attempt to dilute the request.

- We communicate inefficiently by getting the sequence of points backwards.

This is what you can do instead:

- **Check the situation from position 3.** Is the request reasonable? If it is a work request, is what you are about to ask acceptable? If it is a personal request and the situation were reversed, would you feel it acceptable to be asked by the other person? Remember, too, that in many situations, you have a right to ask for help but the other person probably has a right to decline. That's only fair. Another point worth highlighting is that, in many situations, people actually like to help others; it makes them feel good about themselves. Put these two points together and any reluctance to make a request soon evaporates.

- **Consider your words before you start speaking.** In the fewest number of words that will communicate clearly, what do you want and why do you want it? The 'fewest number of words' is important; it will stop you a) beating about the bush and b) unnecessarily apologising. After all, the other person might feel that your request is perfectly ok - until you start telling them how sorry you are and how you know it is an imposition and how they are already very busy, etc. Do we say this to make them feel better about the request? No, perversely, we say it to make ourselves feel better. So be concise.

- **Get the sequence of points right.** If you say, *'I need to ask you for the third quarter figures* [point 1] *and I need them this afternoon* [point 2]. *I'm writing a paper for the chief executive* [point 3] *and she needs them for a presentation this evening* [point 4]' you are running a risk. This risk comes from two sources. First, you will be speaking much more slowly than the other person's brain is working so, as soon as point 1 leaves your lips, the other person's thoughts go into overdrive and, as a result, they may not listen to the points that support your request. Second, putting your points in this sequence increases the chances that the purpose for which you need the third quarter figures will sound like an excuse. A better sequence would be, *'I'm writing a paper for the chief executive for a presentation she's doing this evening. I'll have to include the third quarter figures and, to meet her deadline, I'll need them this afternoon. Is it possible to let me have them after lunch please?'* This is clear and concise, in a logical sequence and, if delivered with a smile and newsreader body language, will feel much better to you and to the other person.

HANDLE PUT-DOWNS

When our confidence is low we can be very susceptible to put-downs (the sarcastic remarks some people make to win their point or just to feel better about themselves). The remarks are often characterised by:

- **Judgement** rather than observation – They may say, *'That's not good enough'* rather than *'That's not the standard we agreed'*.

- **Personal criticism** rather than behavioural feedback – They may say, *'You lack motivation'* rather than *'You don't appear as enthusiastic as I thought you'd be'*.

- **Exaggeration/generalisation** rather than accuracy – They may say, *'You're always doing it wrong'* rather than *'This is the second time those figures don't add up correctly'*.

- **'Gotcha' questions** rather than genuine questions – They may say, *'Were you really stupid enough to believe that?'* rather than *'What was it that made you believe that?'*

Put-downs can be tricky to handle because they often trigger our fight or flight response. This is why, in the heat of the moment, the right response feels elusive. We know that losing our temper or even responding in kind makes us look too sensitive or immature; being unable to respond spontaneously affects our confidence, affects the respect others have for us and does nothing to 'educate' the person who is putting us down. So here are three safe and easy-to-use behaviours that will help you handle put-downs:

1 Raise your deflector shield

If you have ever seen *'Star Trek'* you will know what a deflector shield is. If you haven't, the television show *'Star Trek'* featured the 'Enterprise', a space craft exploring the universe. Inevitably, every few episodes they came under attack from hostile forces and the Enterprise's captain would give the order *'Deflector shield up'*. The scene would then change to the exterior of the Enterprise and you could see each hostile missile evaporate harmlessly against the invisible deflector shield with a gentle 'puff'.

Imagine if you could raise your own invisible deflector shield half way between you and the person firing the put-downs. Whatever they say encounters the deflector shield and just evaporates – 'puff'. Raising an imaginary, invisible deflector shield may sound simplistic but it works because the put-downs do not get through to your emotions. This means that you remain in control of your emotions.

When you control your emotions,
you control your behaviour.

You are then ready to use one or both of the next behaviours. As you read the examples, you can imagine the put-down in a sarcastic tone of voice but always imagine your response sounding as calm and authoritative as a newsreader.

2 Bounce it back

Reflect the words back to the other person. Continuing the above examples relating to judgement, personal criticism, exaggeration/ generalisation and 'gotcha' questions, when:

- They say, *'That's not good enough'*, you could respond, *'It seems it isn't what you expected'*.

- They say, *'You lack motivation'*, you could respond, *'You were expecting more overt enthusiasm'*.

- They say, *'You're always doing it wrong'*, you could respond, *'You're concerned some of the figures aren't correct'*.

- They say, *'Were you really stupid enough to believe that?'* you could respond, *'I see you weren't convinced'.*

Notice that you are not agreeing, disagreeing, retaliating, justifying or anything else at this stage. You are simply responding quickly (which is what you want to do) by bouncing the other person's words back to them. Rather cleverly, however, you have paraphrased using rational, objective words. Not only is the ball now back in the other person's side of the court, you have also sent them a clear signal that a) you do not respond to put-downs and b) you will not be drawn into a childish slanging match but you are happy to have a rational conversation – and you achieved all that without thinking too hard.

If you want to be a little more assertive, you can use the next response.

3 Probe to help them 'put up or shut up'

A simple question returns the ball to the other person's side of the court with minimal effort from you. So, using the same examples (again, with you being 'newsreader calm') if:

- They say, *'That's not good enough'*, you could respond, *'In what way?'*

- They say, *'You lack motivation'*, you could respond, *'What were you expecting to see, exactly?'*

- They say, *'You're always doing it wrong'*, you could respond, *'In what way would you like it done?'*

- They say, *'Were you really stupid enough to believe that?'* you could respond, *'How do you mean?'*

The benefit of simple questions such as these is that they are quick, easy and require very little conscious thinking from you. From the other person's perspective, however, such simple questions are virtually impossible to resist which means they respond with more information and, while they are talking, you have time to think. If their point is genuine (the figures, for example, are incorrect; they just pointed out that fact sarcastically) you are closer to a rational conversation with them. If their point is a groundless put-down, a simple question shows them that put-downs do not work on you.

Two quick points:

- Whenever we read illustrations like these we naturally recall real people and real situations. You might be lucky and the illustrations will transfer to a real situation without modification. It is more likely, however, that you will have to tailor them to your own situations.

- Remember we communicate a lot of meaning with body language and these illustrations only contain words. Reflect and probe like a newsreader and you will communicate one meaning; reflect and probe with even a hint of anger, sarcasm or retaliation and you will communicate another. Hence, the repeated emphasis on staying 'newsreader calm'.

STAND YOUR GROUND

We come across many situations in which we need to stand our ground. It might be a pushy salesperson, a manipulative friend or a demanding manager. When we give in too easily, our confidence suffers a set-back and we teach people that we are a 'push over'. When we stand our ground, however, we strengthen our confidence and teach people to listen to us. The following four behaviours will help you stand your ground positively.

1 The three-part sentence

As the name suggests, the three-part sentence is a sentence in three parts. (Sometimes it might be a couple of sentences but the three parts will still be evident.) In the first part, you **reflect** or bounce-back, as described above. This lets the other person know you have heard them. In the second part, you **state how you feel**. Note, 'state how you feel' not <u>dramatise</u> how you feel. 'I feel angry' delivered like a calm authoritative newsreader is very different from 'I feel angry' delivered like an over-enthusiastic actor from a television soap opera. This prepares the other person for the third part in which you **state what you want**.

Here are some illustrations using the same put-downs from above. (Remember to imagine a newsreader tone of voice as you respond.)

- They say, *'That's not good enough'*. You could respond, *'It may not be what you were expecting, however, I'm concerned that I didn't understand you. Could we go into more detail about what you feel needs changing?'*

- They say, *'You lack motivation'*. You could respond, *'It sounds like you were expecting more enthusiasm, however, I'm worried that you might feel I lack commitment. I'd like to look at how my actual output matched the client's needs'*.

- They say, *'You're always doing it wrong'*. You could respond, *'I can see the figures could be tighter, however, I feel that in the time available, I did pretty well so I think the effort is worth some recognition'*.

- They say, *'Were you really stupid enough to believe that?'* You could respond, *'It is possible I made the wrong choice, however, I don't think sarcasm will help me get it right next time. If you could be more specific, I'd be grateful'*.

While most people respond well to the three-part sentence, it is not as if a switch has been flicked. What the other person says may still be packaged with an unhelpful tone of voice or impatient manner. They may even continue to be awkward. If so, use *the broken record*.

2 The broken record

If you remember those black vinyl discs with grooves that play music, you will know that when a scratch cuts across the grooves, the needle jumps and the music keeps repeating the same phrase over and over again. That is the gist of the broken record; you repeat the same phrase until the other person listens. It is very useful if you easily give in <u>or</u> if you easily lose your temper. It works like this (as you read the example, imagine the manager speaking aggressively and the staff member staying 'newsreader calm'):

MANAGER. *'That's not good enough'.*

STAFF MEMBER. *'It may not be what you were expecting, however, I'm concerned that I may not have understood you. Could we go into more detail about what you feel needs changing, please?'*

MANAGER. *'I shouldn't need to go into more detail. I don't spoon feed my staff.'*

STAFF MEMBER. *'I know that, however, I'm concerned that I don't understand your feedback, so could we go into more detail about what needs changing?'*

MANAGER. *'At your salary you should be able to work it out.'*

STAFF MEMBER. *'Maybe. However, I'm not clear and I need to be if I'm to get it right. So can we discuss it please?'*

MANAGER. *'This is ridiculous. I don't have time.'*

STAFF MEMBER. *'It will save us both time if I'm clear about what needs to be done. Can we discuss it please?'*

MANAGER. *'Oh...for crying out loud. All right. Look, when you calculate those figures you've got to....'*

It is worth highlighting four points about this illustration.

- First, the manager criticising the figures has agreed (albeit with bad grace) to do what the staff member wants. But they are doing it because the staff member stood his or her ground. Maybe next time, the manager will explain things in more detail right at the beginning.

- Second, unlike a literal broken record, the staff member has paraphrased rather than repeated exactly the same phrase. This ensures that he/she does not sound stubborn - just confident enough to stand up for their rights.

- Third, modelling a newsreader kept the staff member's communication positive.

- Finally, he/she only repeated their point three times. In most conversations that will be enough.

3 How to say 'No'

Saying 'No' can be another aspect of confident behaviour that feels uncomfortable because:

- We can be afraid that we will be perceived as unhelpful and no longer 'accepted' (remember the *effect of evolution* explained in chapter 3). This often causes us to say 'Yes' when it would have been better to say 'No'. It can also cause us to lie by inventing an excuse – and that is usually what it sounds like, an excuse invented on the spur of the moment.

- We think ahead and assume that saying 'No' will negate our right to ask this person for help in the future – the evolutionary 'law of reciprocity'.

- We compare their rights to ours and feel that our right to say 'No' is inferior to their right to ask.

When some objective, position 3, common sense is applied, however, these reasons appear pretty flimsy. If you usually help people, saying 'No' once in a while will not change people's perception of you. Networks of people (work, family, neighbours, friends, etc) involve *overall* interdependence. This remains intact even when sometimes people have to put their own needs first. After all, you have a right (even a responsibility) to consider your own needs too. Sometimes you will put yourself first and sometimes you will put other people first. The key word is 'sometimes'.

At times when you need to say 'No', here are some essential points:

- **Think of alternative ways of saying 'No'.** If we only see two alternatives ('Yes' and 'No') it can be a tough choice. When you have a *range* of alternatives, you can choose the one that feels right for the situation. For example, a range from *'Yes'* to *'No'* could look like this: • *'Yes, I'll do it immediately.'* • *'Yes I can help just as soon as I finish what I'm doing now.'* • *'I can help but only if my manager agrees.'* • *'I'd like to help but I have to finish this other task first. I can, however, show you where to find the information if you need it quickly.'* • *'I'd help if I could, however, I have to finish what I'm doing now so I can't.'* • *'No. I'm sorry, I can't do that.'*

    When you have alternative ways of saying 'No',
    you can select the one that feels ok to say, ok for the
    other person to hear and is honest and fair.

- **Have one genuine reason,** even if it is just because you don't want to, because one strong reason sounds valid; multiple reasons or a fabricated reason sound like excuses. If necessary, reinforce it with the *broken record*.

- **Stay focussed.** Keep the conversation focussed on the fact that you cannot help. Do not over-empathise and get sucked into position 2 where you will be susceptible to emotional blackmail. Use the *three-part sentence* to maintain focus.

- Support what you say with newsreader tone of voice and body language. We humans are adept at picking up 'emotional leakage' into body language. If the other person sees 'newsreader' posture, breathing, voice and eyes they will know you mean what you say.

4 How to disagree

Disagreeing requires a degree of confidence and, again, there is a trick that makes it much easier while also making it more effective. That trick is **sequence**.

'*I disagree with you* [disagreement] *because* [reason]' is not an effective sequence; the word 'disagree' is a negative and unpredictable trigger. As soon as the other person hears it, they could be puzzled as to why you're disagreeing, they could wonder how to counter your disagreement, they could consider how to justify their point more strongly, etc. Even though your reason is about to follow the word 'because', a negative trigger often nudges people out of listening mode.

If, on the other hand, you say, '*Because of* [reason] *I can't agree with you* [disagreement]' what you say sounds far more considered and the other person is much more likely to listen to the whole sentence.

You can even soften the disagreement by encouraging them into position 3. For example, if someone in a meeting says, '*Ok let's all come in at the weekend and get the data transferred over to the new system*', a reasonable way of disagreeing would be, '*I understand how that gets the data transferred with minimum disruption* [you're letting them know you've listened to them] *however, I'm concerned that without IT specialists present, we could make mistakes that will take weeks to unravel* [reason]. *To ensure we get it right, I wonder if we should look at some alternatives* [very soft disagreement and sensible alternative suggestion].' Overall this a) looks less like a disagreement and more like rational analysis and b) it gives everyone room for manoeuvre.

PICK YOURSELF UP AFTER A KNOCK

Knocks and set-backs happen. Some people have difficulty getting up again while others seem to get back on track quickly.

The difference is rarely <u>what happens to them</u> it is <u>the way they choose to respond</u> to what happens.

Here is a seven-step plan you can use to respond positively.

Step 1 - Feel bad for a while

Recognise that if a knock or set-back doesn't make you feel bad:

- it wasn't important,

- you don't realise how serious it is,

- you're not normal.

Feeling bad to a significant knock or set-back is normal. Accept that fact and give yourself permission to feel bad. But:

- Be careful with whom you share feeling bad – if people over-sympathise or sternly tell you to pull yourself together, they could make you feel worse.

- Put a time limit on feeling bad. Whether that is hours or weeks depends on the severity of the situation but a time limit avoids your current bad feeling resetting your mood thermostat and becoming a habit. It also leads naturally to a *temporary frame* – you don't feel ok <u>yet</u>, but <u>you will</u>.

Step 2 - Include 'temporary' in the frame

A surprising number of successful entrepreneurs have been bankrupt but, because they frame bankruptcy as temporary rather than permanent, they filter in solutions and opportunities that the 'permanent framers' miss. Many successful authors, actors, athletes and artists have done the same. When you frame a problem or setback as temporary, you open your filter to useful feedback, solutions and opportunities.

Step 3 - Frame the knock as <u>feedback</u> rather than failure

Failure is final but feedback is a special stepping stone that takes you closer to your goal.

Step 4 - Develop a *position 3* strategy

As a position 3 perspective is wider and more emotionally detached than a position 1 perspective, it is a great place from which to plan how you will use the feedback and move on.

Step 5 - Visualise what you want

As the emotions associated with a knock or set-back 'register' strongly in your brain, negative feelings and images will try to remain in your conscious brain in the same way that a bright light appears to remain in your vision long after it has gone. So replace the negative image with a **strong, detailed** and **vibrant** image of what you want and **how you will feel** when you are bathed in the warm glow of light as you emerge from the tunnel. Initially, the image might be weak and you might struggle to see it clearly but, as you practise, it will become brighter and stronger.

Step 6 - Model 'back on track' feelings and behaviours

Short-circuit the recovery process by modelling. Pretend you are through the tunnel. Feel, think and act like someone who is already back on track. Whenever you do this, no matter how shakily or briefly, you make progress, so do it frequently and it becomes easier.

Step 7 - Develop an emotionally 'nutritious' environment

Reinforce positive feelings and behaviour with positive people, movies, television programmes, books, magazines, music and experiences. Feed your conscious and subconscious brains with the feel-good factor – it's great medicine.

REVIEW AND PREVIEW

Feeling confident and behaving confidently go together like two sides of the same coin. In this chapter, therefore, we have focussed on the essentials of confident communication.

We communicate constantly. We do not have to speak to communicate; our breathing, gaze direction, the pace and purpose with which we move, all communicate something. An important question, therefore, is *do you communicate what you mean to communicate?* After all, communication is not complete until what you transmit has been received, filtered, associated and, finally, given meaning by the recipient.

You can take full responsibility for the overall communication process by making sure that your words and body language combine to maximise the chances of successful communication.

It is much easier to do that when you have the right amount of confidence because, when you feel confident, you find it so much easier to control your thoughts and emotions, select the right words and support them with the right body language. As this can be a lot to think about until it becomes habit, I have only described those tips that offer maximum benefit for minimum effort.

A reasonable question to ask at this stage, however, is what can you do if, despite all these good tips, **someone's behaviour takes you so much by surprise** that your fight or flight response is released too quickly for you to control? That is where the final tip comes in.

EMOTIONS, PAVLOV AND THE RUNAWAY TRAIN

Sudden situations

Some situations present a major challenge. Something in the situation triggers negative emotions and negative emotions usually lead to negative behaviour and a poor outcome.

Advice suggesting that you intervene in the process and convert the negative emotions into positive emotions might be ok when you have time to think; we have covered plenty of tips that will help you do that.

But, what about situations that are serious and, above all, sudden? Another driver has just dented your car reversing in a car park, a family member has unexpectedly blown their top at you or a senior manager has just made a cutting remark as you reach the conclusion of your presentation. In sudden situations like these, you do not have time for a lengthy, conscious intervention because, before you know it, your negative emotions are already hurtling down the track with all the speed and momentum of a runaway train leading straight to the 'train crash' of negative behaviour and a poor outcome.

In situations like these you need something that will affect your negative emotions quickly, effectively and easily.

We can fulfil those criteria if we build on what the brain is already very good at doing:

- responding to a stimulus,

- establishing associations,

- processing emotional thoughts incredibly quickly.

Responding to a stimulus

Brains respond to stimuli very quickly. Put your hand on something hot (stimulus) and you will pull it away (response) in a nanosecond. See something scary (stimulus) and your fight or flight response will kick in (response) equally quickly. Receive a sudden put-down (stimulus) and your negative emotions (response) will follow pretty fast. The Nobel prize-winning psychologist and physician, Ivan Petrovich Pavlov (1849-1936), noticed this stimulus-response process too. As dogs' food was prepared (stimulus), the dogs would salivate (response).

Establishing associations

Pavlov then introduced a second stimulus - a ringing bell. It was not long before the dogs learned to *associate* the bell with food. Pavlov repeated the meal-time bell ringing until the association was programmed into the dogs' brains and he could make the dogs salivate just by ringing the bell. This process of learning to respond to an association is called a *Pavlovian Response.*

With the right intervention, you can set up your own Pavlovian response to handle sudden situations more skilfully. All you have to do is add a little 'larger-than-life' imagery because imagery helps association.

You might, for example, have seen entertainers with mega memories who can memorise incredibly long lists of names, numbers or playing cards. One technique they use is to create a story involving the names, numbers or cards. The story sets up the memory-enhancing associations which are further strengthened with larger-than-life imagery. To really capitalise on our brain's natural capabilities, however, we can go one step further and include *emotions* to create even stronger associations.

Processing emotional thoughts

We know that brains process emotional thoughts much faster than they process rational thoughts. That is why, in sudden situations, trying to rationalise away negative thoughts will not work; it is too slow.

> *The best way to tackle negative emotions is with stronger, positive emotions.*

My suggestion is that if, in a sudden situation, your negative emotions are already hurtling down the track with the speed and momentum of a runaway train, you might as well use this larger-than-life imagery to your advantage and create an appropriate, emotionally-charged, association.

The runaway train

All you have to do is associate the sudden release of negative emotions with the runaway train, switch the points and divert the negative emotions off the main track. This takes a split second and enables you to remain cool and calm enough to 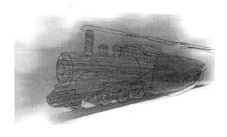 stay focused and get closer to the outcome you want. To work efficiently, however, the runaway train imagery needs a bit more emotion attached to it.

So let's imagine a movie in which there is a runaway train (your emotions). Everyone on the train is unconscious and the train is hurtling down the track at ever increasing speed. As if that wasn't bad enough, farther along the track is a broken down passenger train. (Let's add some drama shall we? The runaway train contains a nuclear weapon, incurable virus or some other devastating device and the immobilised train is full of children, all the doors are locked and a famous actress is dressed as a nun, singing as she plays guitar to keep the children calm.) Every attempt to stop the runaway train has failed but, despite severe injuries and extreme hardship, the star of the movie (you) manages to locate some old rusty, long-forgotten points and, at the very last second, you manage to switch the points and divert the runaway train (your negative emotions) onto a disused track where it can slow down easily and everyone is safe.

That is what you do – you set up a Pavlovian response pre-prepared for sudden situations but, instead of being a full length movie, you sense the train and switch the points in less than a second.

In less than a second, your negative emotions have come and gone. Your thinking is agile and you are resourceful.

There is only one question left – hopefully, you will not encounter serious, sudden situations frequently, so how can you repeat this association often enough to reprogram your brain neurons so that the 'trick' becomes habit? The answer is to repeat the process again and again *in your imagination.*

Imagination, repetition and brain neurons

We know that repetition is a very effective way of reprogramming brain neurons – that is how you became fluent at changing gear in your car, tying your shoe laces and brushing your teeth. What we don't always realise is that *imaginary practice* is also an effective way of reprogramming brain neurons - your brain actually 'experiences' the event, including the emotions, as if you were actually doing it.

When you practise something frequently and intensely in your imagination, you stimulate the same neuronal pathways that you stimulate when you practise physically.

Successful athletes, racing car drivers, actors and musicians include imaginary rehearsals in their preparation; it is that effective. You can do it too by 'experiencing' the imagery and the Pavlovian response repeatedly in your imagination.

This way it will happen easily, exactly when you need it.

WHAT TO DO NEXT

Hopefully this chapter has given you a lot of ideas that will help you behave confidently. Smiling, walking with purpose, making eye contact and adopting newsreader body language are easy and effective ways to start. Modelling (specific and general) is another quick and effective idea. Making small talk with strangers and making requests will help your confidence grow. From there it is a relatively small step to handling put-downs, standing your ground, saying 'No' and disagreeing skilfully. These ideas combine into a powerful resource with which you can pick yourself up after a knock. You can even program your brain to respond positively in serious, sudden situations.

As you choose the ideas about which you feel most enthusiastic and combine them with some of the thinking tips from the previous chapter, you have a powerful, confidence-building combination. It is a combination that you, and people around you, will notice.

You will even be able to use it to help other people.

Chapter 6

How to be a radiator rather than a drain

IS THIS YOU?

Have you noticed that some people have an uplifting effect on other people's moods and some people have a depressing effect on the moods of those around them? Who would you rather be with, the mood lifters or mood depressors? What effect would you like to have on other people? Have you ever wondered how self-confidence makes you better company?

IN THIS CHAPTER

As confidence enables you to enhance the quality of the relationships you enjoy, this chapter will help you:

- Make other people feel good (balancing the natural focus on 'self' in 'self-confident').

- Practise *quietly confident* behaviours that are respected and appreciated by others.

- Attract positive behaviour from other people (because what goes around comes around).

It all comes from being a *radiator* rather than a *drain*.

A THOUGHT-PROVOKING STORY

A course participant told me a story that made me think.

A friend of hers was in a long-term relationship with a live-in boyfriend. Unfortunately, the boyfriend was a 'glass half empty' person. In fact, that's a bit too generous; his 'half empty' glass hadn't been washed properly and had a crack in it. Nothing was ever right or as good as it 'should' be. There was always a downside or a 'Yes, but'. He never had any luck and when he did try something, it was 'difficult' and 'probably wouldn't work'. The boyfriend was a significant part of the friend's 'environment' and, as we are all susceptible to the messages we receive from our environment, his moods and behaviour began to have a negative, cumulative effect on her. One day at work, during an informal review, she looked depressed enough for her manager to ask what was wrong. This question opened the emotional flood gates and the friend explained how her boyfriend's persistently pessimistic behaviour was depressing her. Apparently, the manager listened without interruption for fifteen minutes until she was sure the friend had finished and then simply said, *'There are two types of people in this world, radiators and drains'*. And that was all she said.

With that simple statement, the friend was nudged into position 3 and realised what was happening. According to the course participant who was telling me the story, the friend dumped the 'drain', found a guy who was a genuine 'radiator' and every aspect of her life improved.

People, and our relationships with them, are such a huge part of our environment that, when we are influenced too much by drain behaviour, it really affects us. Conversely, when we are exposed to radiator behaviour, it has a beneficial effect on us.

The more positive behaviour you radiate to others,
the more they enjoy being with you.

There is just something about drain behaviour we dislike and something about radiator behaviour that we truly value.

In the same way that a heating system's radiator spreads warmth, when a person acts as a radiator, a personal warmth radiates from them benefiting all those who are near. Once we associate someone with radiator behaviour, a Pavlovian response ensures that even their simple presence can lighten our mood and make us feel good. This contrasts dramatically with 'drains' whose behaviour (and sometimes even just their presence) acts like a black hole on cheerfulness, optimism and confidence.

So, before we look at radiator behaviour, let's look at drain behaviour to avoid.

THE DRAIN BRAIN AND DRAIN BEHAVIOUR

The negative paradigms and programs running in a drain's brain make it easy for their filter to delete or distort good things and to filter in and generalise bad things. Their glass is half empty rather than half full. They seek environmental reinforcement of their paradigms and programs by paying attention to newspaper articles and television programmes that  confirm the accuracy of their negative view. They associate with people who like nothing better than to whinge and moan. They benefit from the pay-off of gaining confirmation that their negative views are correct and, as fate will not let them succeed, they have no need to expend effort or take risks trying.

The negative cycle continues and they play 'games' as they interact with others. A favourite game is the 'no win' or 'what's the point' game, illustrated by this dialogue.

> DRAIN. 'I haven't got any friends.'

> COLLEAGUE. 'Why don't you go out a bit more and meet some?'

DRAIN. 'I don't know where to go.'

COLLEAGUE. 'Why not start playing tennis again and join a club? You used to enjoy tennis and you'd make lots of new friends there.'

DRAIN. 'I haven't played for so long, everyone will beat me.'

COLLEAGUE. 'Yes, but only to begin with. You'll soon pick it up again.'

DRAIN. 'Even if I do, I'm not fit enough to beat the younger players.'

COLLEAGUE. 'Then play some of the veterans while you get your fitness back.'

DRAIN. 'I've got nothing in common with old people.'

COLLEAGUE. 'But you'll meet some younger people in the club house.'

DRAIN. 'People normally go there with their friends.'

COLLEAGUE. 'Well...why don't you go with a friend?'

DRAIN. 'I haven't got any friends.'

No matter what well-meaning suggestions the colleague makes, this 'game' ensures he or she won't win.

In addition to 'games', Drains also use:

Comparing. Reference groups to whom they compare themselves are better at things, learn things more easily, are luckier, more fortunate, more favoured, etc. Their comparisons are never favourable.

DRAIN (WATCHING A FOOTBALL MATCH). 'I'm useless at football compared to those guys.'

COLLEAGUE. 'They're professionals. They probably practise forty hours a week.'

DRAIN. 'Yes, but they've got natural talent. Even if I practised fifty hours a week I'd still be useless.'

Competing. Any attempts by others at empathising with the drain person are always beaten.

DRAIN. 'I had a dreadful night's sleep.'

COLLEAGUE. 'I didn't sleep too well either. It was so hot and humid.'

DRAIN. 'Yes but I didn't sleep <u>at all</u>.'

Criticising. When a drain feels bad they can relieve the feeling slightly by highlighting how bad everyone and everything else is, will be or might be.

COLLEAGUE. 'Isn't the weather lovely?'

DRAIN. 'Only because we're at work. I bet it will rain at the weekend.'

RADIATOR BEHAVIOUR

Radiator behaviour, however, is far more positive. It has two main characteristics – making people feel good and genuinely listening to them.

Making people feel good

Radiators seem to understand instinctively that brains process feelings faster than facts and so they:

- Display simple body language, such as a smile and eye contact to make us feel welcome and included.

- Use their posture, breathing and pace (think relaxed newsreader) to signal that they are attentive to us and enjoying our company.

Genuinely listening to people

Radiators are very 'other person' focussed. They are less concerned with telling us how they feel or what they have been doing and more interested in finding out how we feel and what we have been doing. This makes them good listeners – and, remember, we really value good listeners.

Skilled listening is not as easy as it sounds. It involves far more than simply keeping quiet and mumbling, *'Mmmm'*, *'Wow'* and *'Did you really?'* every now and again. You can tell when someone is listening because they are very focussed on the listener. They don't make judgmental comments or hijack the conversation with their own stories. They often probe to find out more and summarise to check they understand.

Consciously making other people feel good by genuinely listening to them increases your radiator behaviour, especially when you are responding to other people's drain behaviour.

RESPONDING TO OTHER PEOPLE'S DRAIN BEHAVIOUR

The description of drain behaviour might have reminded you of people you know. They might be people with whom you work, live or associate and you cannot, or do not want to, avoid their company. What you really want to do is convert their negativity into something more positive.

The tool with which you can do this is your behaviour.

The first point is what *not* to do. It is very tempting to go with the flow and benignly agree with them or even sympathise. This will condone and reinforce their behaviour, effectively encouraging more of it. It might also be tempting to confront them and bluntly point out how negative they are. This will also reinforce their negative perspective because what will get through their filter is that even you are against them.

You need to be subtle, gradually encouraging them to shift their perspective and the best way of doing that is *probing*.

DRAIN. 'I haven't got any friends.'

RADIATOR. 'How do you mean?'

DRAIN. 'I've lost touch with most of the people I used to know and the others all seem to be too busy.'

RADIATOR. 'How do you feel about the situation?'

DRAIN. 'Well...a bit sad I suppose.'

RADIATOR. 'How would you like the situation to be different?'

DRAIN. 'I'd like to get out more. Have more of a social life.'

RADIATOR. 'That sounds good. In your mind's eye, what specifically can you see yourself doing with friends?'

DRAIN. 'Er...possibly playing tennis, having a beer afterwards. That kind of thing.'

Probing a drain will not always be this easy. After all, the first response they want is confirmation that the situation is negative and, when they don't get that response, they may try harder and be even more negative. If you continue to respond with probing, however, they will gradually get the message that you will not join in the negativity; in fact, being negative with you doesn't have the satisfactory pay-off for them that they were expecting and, without a satisfactory pay-off, their behaviour will gradually change.

It is worth highlighting, however, exactly what you have done in this dialogue. Not only have you avoided agreeing, sympathising or disagreeing with the drain, you have also avoided a) exploring why he or she has no friends (just like asking the wrong question, the subconscious will find reasons) and b) offering solutions (which will trigger the 'no win' game).

Instead you have encouraged participation (*'How do you mean?'*), tested motivation (*'How do you feel about the situation?'*) and encouraged visualisation of outcomes (*'How would you like the situation to be different?'*) and (*'That sounds good. In your mind's eye, what specifically can you see yourself doing with friends?'*). That word 'specifically' is especially valuable at this stage of the conversation. Once you have built up rapport and momentum in a conversation, the other person hardly notices words like specifically, exactly and precisely but subconsciously, they respond by being more *specific*, *exact* and *precise*. In this way, you make the outcome more vivid, real and tangible. Then, and only then, you can start to explore options.

> RADIATOR. *'That sounds good. In your mind's eye, what specifically can you see yourself doing with friends?'*

> DRAIN. *'Er...possibly playing tennis, having a beer afterwards. That kind of thing.'*

> RADIATOR. *'What, precisely, is it about tennis and a beer that you like?'*

> DRAIN. *'It's good exercise, fun and afterwards you have something to talk about even if you've never met the other person before.'*

RADIATOR. 'So, if you knew someone who was keen to start playing tennis again, what suggestions would you make to them?'

DRAIN. 'I'd tell them to join a club, have a few lessons and join the league.'

RADIATOR. 'And if they said, "Yes but I won't know anyone" exactly what would you say to encourage them?'

DRAIN. 'I'd tell them they don't have to know anyone. Joining the league means matches are arranged easily and after a month or two they'll know lots of people.'

Notice that options were also explored subtly. *'So, if you knew someone who was keen to start playing tennis again, what suggestions would you make to them?'* is the kind of question that can only be answered from position 3 which, you will recall from Chapter 4, has a wider perspective and less *emotional attachment* than positions 1 or 2. *'And if they said, "Yes but I won't know anyone" exactly what would you say to encourage them?'* is a clever bit of probing because, when the conversation moves to the stage where you suggest they can do that too, they can only resist by going against their own logic. In response to your probing, they have effectively rehearsed what you want them to say.

A final point - subtle probing needs to be just that – **subtle**. Questions like, *'Can you tell me what, precisely, you like about tennis'* and *'Don't you agree that by playing tennis you'll meet lots of people'* kill the rapport that is essential for conversations like this to work. When people begin a question, *'Can you tell me'*, it is a clear signal that they are deploying a technique. (Think about it, when you meet a colleague on Monday morning do you ask, *'Can you tell me, did you have a good weekend?'* or just *'Did you have a good weekend?'* The former sounds strangely formal but the latter sounds natural. Similarly, in a normal conversation would you ask, *'What do you think of the weather?'* or *'Don't you agree with me that the weather is nice?'* The first question shows you are interested in what *they* think; the second question shows you are more interested in confirming that they *think like you*.)

SUMMARY

In summary, drain behaviour is not nice and is best avoided. One option is to stay away from the people themselves but sometimes that is neither possible nor desirable. The alternative, therefore, is to modify their behaviour and the best way of doing that is with subtle probing. This is the most effective way of helping them and making them better to be with. In doing so, your radiator behaviour shines through, helping them.

You benefit in two ways. First, as *what goes around comes around*, you will receive positive behaviour from others. Second, as you reflect on your helpful behaviour, you will feel better about yourself; you will justifiably feel more confident.

It's a cumulative process.

Chapter 7

Magnificent you

THIS IS YOU

I hope you have enjoyed learning about all the ways in which you can think, feel and behave more confidently.

I hope you feel optimistic about putting the tips into practice and can already feel a change taking place. You and other people will appreciate the difference.

There is just one remaining question, how can you make what you have learned a **way of life**?

WHAT ARE YOU BECOMING?

None of us can ever avoid the fact that we are changing. The relentless passage of time, maturity, ageing and experience of events ensures that change. (By the way, I would encourage you to be unconcerned about ageing. Just remember, *'Getting older isn't so bad when you consider the alternative'*.)

I would, however, encourage you to be very aware of the events in your life and how you choose to experience them – that is, how you think about them. The effect of the vast majority of events is slow, subtle and **cumulative**.

> *Many changes creep up on us slowly and only show themselves with enough passage of time for their effects to be evident with hindsight.*

If you are relatively old, you might have had that sobering experience of seeing a photograph of your younger self and wondering where all the years went. If you are relatively young, look at the older people around you; they once had your fitness, strength, energy, humour, hopes, ambitions and dreams.

It's an old saying that today is the first day of the rest of our life. It's a true one too.

QUIET CONFIDENCE AND THE CUMULATIVE EFFECT

So, what is your future? What are you becoming? When your day-to-day responses to everyday people and events are underpinned by quiet confidence, what will be the positive cumulative effect on your life and those around you? When:

- you genuinely feel and look more confident,

- your thinking is confident and rooted in objective reality,

- your internal and external benchmarks are healthy,

your everyday responses change. The cumulative effect is positive. You find it easy and natural to be positive.

Being positive is not about seeing everything through rosy spectacles (that is being unrealistic.) Being positive means:

- **Filtering in opportunities.** Drains wouldn't spot an opportunity if it bit them on the nose. Radiators, perhaps because they are less self-obsessed and more outwardly focussed, spot opportunities. It might be an interesting person to talk to, a promotion possibility or an opportunity to help someone.

- **Having a positive expectation.** As soon as an Olympic high jumper expects to fail, that is usually what they do. When they expect to clear the bar they *give themselves a sporting chance.* A common trait of successful entrepreneurs is that they expect to succeed. What do free-style rock climbers expect to do, fall or reach the top safely?

Whether you are meeting friends for coffee, solving a complex problem or being interviewed for the job of your dreams, a positive expectation gives you a sporting chance.

- **Having a 'forward-looking' approach to problems.** If positive thinking was all that success required, most of us would be rich. It is a good start but we also need to be objectively realistic about the obstacles and problems we encounter along the way. Some people's paradigms interpret obstacles as insurmountable and they throttle back. Radiators anticipate and plan. John Paul Getty was once asked to what he attributed his success in business. He replied that, in every venture, he thought of everything that could go wrong and then made sure it didn't. NASA astronauts constantly ask, *'What's the next thing that could kill us?'* Then they make sure it doesn't. We all encounter problems - it is how we predict and respond that illustrates the paradigms and programs at play.

- **Distinguishing between failure and feedback.** It is not only problems that stop drains in their tracks; drains filter failure as final. Failure associates with, and confirms, their negative programs. Radiators, on the other hand, filter failure as feedback. They reflect on it (from position 3) and use that information to move on. JK Rowling's first Harry Potter novel was rejected by twelve publishers. Walt Disney was rejected by over 300 banks before he found one that agreed a loan to build his theme park. James Dyson famously had over 5,000 setbacks before his cyclone vacuum cleaner worked to his satisfaction. Failure provides valuable information that helps us move closer to what we want.

The key to success is less what happens to you and more how you respond to what happens to you.

That is especially true when events do not unfold as we hoped.

It is possible that some people reading this chapter will think, *'Yeah, all this radiator stuff, thinking positively, seeing feedback rather than failure is ok with small problems but it won't work for big ones'.* Won't it? Let's see. Here are two thought-provoking examples illustrating the effect of our thinking - one negative and one positive. Both true.

Example 1

The first example concerns a participant on a course I was running many, many years ago. Everyone introduced themselves at the start of the course. Inevitably some people went into more detail than others and you could tell from their tone and pace that some were looking forward to the course. One participant, however, introduced himself by saying that he had been with this organisation for three years. His whole demeanour communicated negativity. He went on to say that, before this job, he had a career with a major organisation until they 'rationalised' and, as he put it, 'Threw me onto the scrapheap'. His tone and body language told all his colleagues he felt he was still on the 'scrapheap'. In fact, they, and the organisation for which they were proud to work, was part of his 'scrapheap'. This is hardly a way to win friends and influence people; neither is it a way to enjoy getting up in the morning and going to work.

Being made redundant was something that happened to him - that is fact. Being 'on the scrapheap' is not fact, it is perception. Feeling that way three years later is habit.

Over the years I have met many people who, after leaving school or college, had joined an employer and had assumed that they would have a good, secure, long term career - only to be made redundant in their 30s, 40s or 50s. The vast majority all said that, once they had recovered from the shock, they learned from it and found a job that provided more satisfaction and better work/life balance. The 'scrapheap' on which this course participant felt he resided was entirely of his own making.

Example 2

The second example concerns a man I know who was not only a keen golfer but also in the early stages of what would have been a promising career. He then discovered he had the incurable, deteriorative, muscle-wasting disease, muscular dystrophy. This was a life-changing event far bigger than being made redundant. He was no longer able to play golf, continue his career and, in time, even walk unaided. The simple, everyday actions that most of us take for granted, presented him with a huge challenge. He had every right to be negative but that would have made the situation worse. Many people would have been resigned to spending the rest of their lives on the 'scrapheap' but, he is a radiator. What did he do? He established a national charity to raise money for children and young people suffering from the same debilitating condition. To raise money, he needed publicity and, in 2004, he became the first and, at the time of writing, the only disabled person to have successfully led expeditions to both the North and South Poles. To emphasise the enormity of this challenge, I once saw him give a presentation about his polar achievements; two strong men were needed to help him out of his wheelchair and climb three steps to the lectern.

His life credo, *Quant Je Puis* ('As Much as I Can') underpins a disability (or disABILITY as he prefers to frame it) that will never define him; a disability that has become a passport enabling him to influence and inspire others. His vision, courage and determination are truly inspiring.

That he has muscular dystrophy is fact. Deciding to do something that will help others 'less fortunate' is perception. Being an inspiration to others, despite natural modesty, has become a habit. (If you want to be inspired, 'Google' *Michael McGrath* and the *Muscle Help Foundation*.)

Hopefully, major challenges like redundancy or ill health will not affect you. Like the majority of people, it is the cumulative effect of your responses to life's everyday challenges that will determine whether your future is good or bad.

All you have to do to make the cumulative effect work for you is choose the tips from this book that register with you most and put them into practice until they become habit.

HABIT

Habit is very useful to us. Due to the limited capacity of the conscious brain, most of our thoughts and behaviours are habit. When we are learning something new, we have to think about it consciously. We cannot say we have truly learned it until we can do it without consciously thinking about it – that is, we have only really learned the activity when it is embedded in our subconscious as habit.

Our goal when learning about confidence is to help new ways of thinking and new behaviours transfer from the conscious, where they can feel unnatural or 'difficult' (like folding your arms the 'wrong' way), to the subconscious where they become habits. As this can be a precarious process, here are three **proven tips** to help you turn what you have learned into natural habits.

1 Rehearse in your imagination

What advice would you give an Olympic weightlifter who repeatedly imagined himself being unable to lift the dumb-bell or a sprinter who repeatedly imagined herself false starting? It's a no-brainer. You would advise them to stop imagining what they *don't want* and start imagining what they *do want* and then rehearse it repeatedly in their imaginations.

Yet what happens to us when our confidence feels low and we have a forthcoming challenge such as a difficult conversation? Our brains default into imagining the problems. When you think about it, however, they are *your* thoughts.

*What you think about and how you think about it are
the two things on this planet over which you can have total
control when you choose to take it.*

You can make that control easier with familiarity. That familiarity can be real or imagined – that is why imaginary dress rehearsals are so effective.

Let's say you have a forthcoming conversation with a difficult colleague. In your imagination, sit in a television studio. You are the producer, director and scriptwriter. In front of you are two actors. One looks like your colleague and the other looks like you. Brief the actor who looks like you. Tell them how you want them to feel, to think and to behave. Shout 'Action' and let them start. As soon as 'your' actor deviates, shout 'Cut', brief him or her again and 'Take 2'. Do as many 'takes' as you like until your actor has got it right. Then 'morph' into the screen and become the actor yourself so that you are now seeing the scene, not through a camera but through your own eyes. Feel, think and behave the way you have just been watching and repeat it again and again until *it feels natural and you can access the imaginary dress rehearsal easily*. You can rehearse like this as often as you like - when you are lying in bed, showering, walking the dog, etc. It works wonderfully.

2 Visit the brain gym for at least four weeks

I have heard that when novices join a gym, most of them last less than two weeks. Why such a brief period? It takes more than two weeks of regular exercise to prepare your body to accept exercise. This is another 'Catch 22' because during those two weeks, the exercise is uncomfortable. Many people frame this discomfort as failure and their mental gremlin presses the replay button on their *'I can't do it'* program, especially if their reference group comprises the regulars who have been going to the gym for years. Consequently, many of them give up, especially those for whom 'getting fit' was a New Year's resolution. Gyms are a lot emptier at the end of January than they are at the beginning of January!

If, however, the new gym-goers used those first two weeks simply to get their bodies accustomed to exercising, keeping the weights and exercises modest, they could then begin 'stretching' themselves in weeks three, four and beyond. They could add a few more kilos to the weights, add a few more repetitions to the exercises and gradually build up, using last month's performance as their reference point. In this way they would stretch themselves and not strain themselves.

By week four, developing their fitness would be fun, effective and, above all, sustained.

This concept also applies to exercising one's brain. It may take you a couple of weeks to get your brain accustomed to thinking differently, so keep the new thoughts close to the edge of your comfort zone because, in those weeks, thinking differently will feel as 'wrong' as folding your arms the other way round. You can then begin 'stretching' yourself, deliberately stepping outside your comfort zone, noticing how much more positively you are thinking. By **week four**, you will be ready for bigger challenges and you can really stretch out.

You might also recognise and accept four important points about learning:

- **Most worthwhile learning opportunities are just outside, rather than inside, your comfort zone.** Like playing sport against someone a bit better than you are, it improves your game by stretching you. Your comfort zone expands, encompassing more of what, not so long ago, would have made you uncomfortable. Now it's easy.

- Performing just outside your comfort zone can feel uncomfortable. If you frame discomfort in that situation as something to be avoided, you will probably throttle back and fail. **When you frame this discomfort as proof you are learning, it becomes stimulating and invigorating.**

- Learning by stretching (not straining) yourself just outside your comfort zone results in some failure as well as some success. **Just like learning to walk, however, the ratio between success and failure improves and pretty soon you will feel ready to move up a gear** and step outside your growing comfort zone again and again, enlarging it each time.

- **You choose when you have reached your personal 'cruising altitude'.** Some people want to play tennis sufficiently well to have an enjoyable knock-about with friends, others want to do well in the local amateur league and others want to play professionally. It is the same with confidence. Whether you want to get to watch your favourite television programme occasionally, apply for promotion at work or run for president/ prime minister, you can choose when it's time to 'unfasten your seat belt' and relax.

The one proviso I would put on this last point is that most people have more potential than they realise. Just imagine if a magic genie promised you that whatever you aimed for (as long as it was legal and moral) you would achieve. Wouldn't you aim higher? So don't accept a lower 'cruising altitude' than you deserve.

If you reach for the stars and miss, you still have
a handful of beautiful sky.

3 Choose and practise happy responses to get the happy habit

Positive psychologists have told us for a long time that happiness is less a consequence of events and more a consequence of the way we respond to events. As we have seen in this book, responses rooted in quiet confidence are positive and empowering responses. So, as we can choose our responses, we can choose confident responses and, effectively, choose happiness.

Making that choice all day and every day, however, will tie up a lot of conscious thinking. What we need, therefore, is *the happy habit*. How do you develop a habit? The most proven way is repetition, repetition, repetition.

In the same way that a tennis player will repeat strokes until they become habit, a musician will repeat scales until they become habit and anyone learning a foreign language will repeat words until they become habit, we need to repeat happy, confident responses until they become habit.

Practise 'happy' and you will get the happy habit and
that habit will open up a new world for you.

DISCOVERING NEW LANDS

Even at this stage, you may find your mental gremlin trying to divert you from becoming happy and confident, so remember the old saying,

You cannot discover new lands if you are afraid
to lose sight of the shore.

The trick is not to be unafraid when losing sight of the shore but to recognise that fear is nature's way of suggesting you take care, assess risk accurately, prepare for problems and ensure you have the resources to tackle them. You can redefine 'fear' and make it situation-specific. If your car lurches uncontrollably on a narrow, icy road it is scary. If you are on a roller coaster, the same sensation is exhilarating. Sweating in a meeting is unwelcome; sweating in a gym is proof the exercise is beneficial.

THE TIPPING POINT

If you want to learn a few helpful phrases in a foreign language, it will take a little effort. If you want to become fluent in that language it will take a disproportionate amount of hard work. If you want to get a bit fitter, it will take a little effort. If you want to win an international body building competition, you will have to put in a disproportionately immense amount of effort. Getting better at some things requires an exponential increase in effort.

Learning to be more confident is not like that at all; it does more than get easier – it gets <u>disproportionately easier.</u>

Due to the interplay between confident thinking and confident behaviour, the chicken and egg process works for you so efficiently that you suddenly notice exponential improvements for less effort and, just like adding grains of rice to scales, the cumulative effect soon takes you past the tipping point. Bingo! You are closer to getting the life you want.

WHAT DO YOU WANT
(REALLY, REALLY WANT)?

As you approach the end of this book, I hope this is a question you will think about - what do you want - *really, really want?*

We have covered a lot of ground in this book. Throughout, I have tried to make it a *how to* book and to explain the tried and tested tips it contains in easy-to-understand terms with which everyone can feel comfortable. My intention has been to have a positive effect on your ability to handle life's 'snakes and ladders' and to enjoy 'radiator' relationships with people who matter to you and, of course, that includes your relationship with yourself. In this way, no matter how good the quality of your life now, it improves even further.

To achieve that improvement, you can look at the tips and select your personal favourites, focussing on those that will make the way you think and the way you behave mutually supportive. That way you benefit from the positive 'chicken and egg' spiral.

Making your thinking work for you is probably more challenging than making your behaviour work for you because most of your confidence-related thinking is subconscious. As you apply your selection of tips, however, you will find it progressively easier to clean up your paradigms and programs, deleting any (probably installed during childhood) that are now long past their use-by date. You will also find it progressively easier to assess risk accurately, keeping your evolutionary survival responses alert for when you need them and in the background when you don't. This will enable you to see reality more accurately through an objective, 'position 3' filter. This will apply to both the reality that is 'out there' and, just like riding a bike, to the reality of your own potential.

Controlling the constant, and basically well-meaning, chatter from your mental gremlin is a great feeling. Turning your self-talk into a mental mentor is an even better one. It is also an accurate indicator that the 'polarity' of your chicken and egg spiral is positive more of the time, that your 'state' is positive and that your 'mood thermostat' is in radiator territory.

It is not long before the daily cumulative effect reaches the tipping point and you know you are thinking, feeling and communicating calmly and confidently in situations that matter to you. You also know that you will continue thinking, feeling and communicating this way for the rest of your life.

This is important because a lot of literature on positive thinking and self-improvement and even the western 'success culture' tells us that we should have goals. We are told that, without a goal, we won't know where we are going and, consequently, we may go in the wrong direction and end up somewhere else. Sometimes that is relevant and at other times it is totally misleading.

If you read books by great travel writers, they write about the journey, not about the destination. One of my favourite travel books is Ted Simon's *Jupiter's Travels* recounting his four-year solo journey around the world by motorbike in the 1970s.

He describes the breakdowns, the accidents and even being arrested as *the real journey* because it is then that you meet the people, make the friends, establish the relationships and, in essence, have the experiences that mean much, much more than reaching the journey's destination.

So this question, *'What do you want (really, really want)?'* is less about where you want to go and more about how much you want to enjoy the journey - the events, the experiences, the friends and the relationships.

My recommendation is that you do not think of confidence as a goal; think of it as part of a process. That process is your growth and development as a human being. Confidence is the vehicle that takes you forward.

Enjoy the journey.

Chapter 8

Final thoughts

OVERVIEW

Often, I find that when reading books and articles or listening to conference speakers, certain things register with me. Hopefully, as you have read this book, certain things will have registered with you too. Continuing that theme, I thought I would finish with a few of my favourite things people have said.

The first list is a list of things people have said that, with the benefit of hindsight, have not just proved to be wrong but very wrong indeed! They illustrate what happens so easily when we encounter something contrary to our current paradigms.

THINGS PEOPLE HAVE SAID THAT PROVED TO BE WRONG

'X-rays are clearly a hoax.' (Lord Kelvin, 1896, President of the Royal Society, UK, and, at the time, Britain's foremost scientist.)

'No aeroplane will ever be practically successful.' (Lord Kelvin again, 1902.)

'When the Paris Exhibition closes, electric light will close with it and no more will be heard of it.' (Erasmus Wilson, Professor at Oxford University, UK, in 1878.)

'I just don't see a future for it.' (Leo Fender's business partner just before he quit. Leo Fender continued to pursue his design for the electric guitar. The Fender Music Corporation now not only makes and sells 200,000 electric guitars a year but the original 1954 design of the Fender Stratocaster is the most instantly recognised and copied electric guitar in history.)

'That rainbow song's no good. Take it out.' (Instruction in a memo from an MGM executive after the first screening of *The*

Wizard of Oz.) Incidentally, another film executive tried to cut Audrey Hepburn singing *Moon River* from *Breakfast at Tiffany's.*

'You ought to go back to driving a truck.' (Concert hall manager firing Elvis Presley in 1954.) Buddy Holly received even more cutting criticism at the start of his tragically brief career.

'Very interesting, my boy, but it will never work.' (Professor of Aeronautical Engineering at Cambridge University, UK, when Frank Whittle showed him his plans for the jet engine.)

'There is a world market for, maybe, five computers.' (Thomas Watson, Chairman of IBM, 1943.)

'There is no significant market for it.' (The response Chester Carlson received from IBM, General Electric and other companies, 1939-44, when he tried to interest them in his newly invented photocopying machine. It was eventually taken up by Xerox.)

'If this goes *really* well, we could end up employing as many as 30 people.' (Bill Gates to his business partner, Paul Allen, after a meeting with IBM to discuss supplying MSDOS, 1980.)

'I can't do it.' (Most of us at some stage when learning something new.)

AND NOW FOR SOME POSITIVE SAYINGS

The only way to guarantee that you never win the lottery is never to buy a ticket. When you do buy one, **you are guaranteed the same chance as everyone else.**

Like many people, you probably hinder your own performance. When you bypass your mental gremlin, you will find **success comes more easily.**

Personality is rarely an issue because, like everyone else, you have many different aspects to your mental makeup. *Flexible thinking* **is what makes the most difference** because when you are mentally agile you can access the internal resources you need, when you need them.

Failure is only final when you incorrectly frame feedback. **Reframe feedback and failure becomes a stepping stone.**

It's amazing what you can do when you forget you can't do it.

When you **change the way you think,** you **change the way you behave.** You can no more stop it changing than you can keep your eyes open when you sneeze.

If you want to make room in your wardrobe for new clothes you have to get rid of some old ones. The same applies to **new behaviours** in your life and **new thoughts** in your brain.

Your thoughts are the one thing on this planet you can control when you choose to. All it takes is a little practice. Your feelings are the manifestation of your thoughts. Therefore you can **choose your feelings.**

Repeated conscious thoughts change subconscious programs, resetting your mental sat-nav and mood thermostat. Once **reset**, they will not argue; they will act as programmed.

When you take an activity you can already do and add a little 'stretch', you **expand your comfort zone**.

Good ideas only have to work some of the time to get you **closer to the outcomes you want** more of the time.

What you think about and *how* you think about it determine the way you experience life and, consequently, they affect the **quality of your life.**

If at first you don't succeed...*just **get on with it***. (Isn't that what you did when you were learning to walk?)

'I'll believe it when I see it.' Perhaps, but sometimes **believing it makes it easier** to see.

ACKNOWLEDGEMENTS

Thanks to:

My good friends Carol Bennitt, Helen Emanuel and Krista Powell Edwards for their helpful and thorough feedback on an early draft.

Andrea Brajnovic for the illustrations. www.andreabrajnovic.com.

Rosy Apps for the diagrams. www.rosieapps.com.

John Ohle Photography for permission to use the photograph on the back cover.

Michael McGrath for permission to write about him in the chapter 'Magnificent You'. You can learn more about this incredible man and his charitable work at http://www.michaelmcgrath.co.uk/ and http://www.musclehelp.com/.

Ted Simon for permission to write about him and use his picture in the chapter 'Magnificent You'. You can learn more about Ted's travels, his wonderful writing and his foundation at http://jupitalia.com/.

END NOTE

Thank you for buying Quietly Confident.

I hope you have enjoyed reading it as much as I have enjoyed writing it. If you feel motivated to do so, I am always very grateful to everyone who leaves a positive review.

If you would like to pursue any of the ideas in *Quietly Confident*, or let me know how you are getting on with the ideas and suggestions in it, please feel free to email me at <u>terry@terrygillen.net</u>

46115784R00083

Printed in Poland
by Amazon Fulfillment
Poland Sp. z o.o., Wrocław